COMMUNIST CHINA'S
FOREIGN POLICY

COMMUNIST
CHINA'S FOREIGN
POLICY

R. G. BOYD

FREDERICK A. PRAEGER, *Publisher*

New York

BOOKS THAT MATTER

Published in the United States of America in 1962 by
Frederick A. Praeger, Inc., Publisher
64 University Place, New York 3, N.Y.

Library of Congress Catalog Card Number: 62-13750

COMMUNIST CHINA'S FOREIGN POLICY is published in two editions:
A Praeger Paperback (PPS-76)
A clothbound edition

This book is Number 107 in the series of
Praeger Publications in Russian History and World Communism

Printed in the United States of America

TO THE PEOPLE OF CHINA,

THE ENDURING, THE MISGUIDED,

AND ESPECIALLY

THE COURAGEOUS ONES

Contents

Preface

This work is based on research undertaken in the Department of International Relations at the Institute of Advanced Studies in the Australian National University during 1959-61. The final draft was written during the first half of 1961, when much speculation had begun about the future of China's relations with the Soviet Union. The author hopes that he has made some contribution to Western and free Asian understanding of the alliance between these two leading Communist powers.

The use of the word "China" throughout the text is not to be taken as a criticism of the position of the Chinese Nationalist Government on Taiwan, or as an implied plea for wider official recognition of the Chinese Communist government. The formal title of the Chinese Communist regime, viz., the Chinese Peoples Republic, is not used.

Western policies towards the Chinese Communist government are considered in the final chapter. It has been the author's intention to assess first the outlook and objectives of the Chinese Communist system.

In the notes, the official Chinese Communist information service, the New China News Agency, is referred to by the customary abbreviation, NCNA.

CHAPTER 1

Emergence

The establishment of a Communist state in China and its emergence as a strong power in Asia resulted from events which developed out of the situation in the Far East at the end of the First World War. China was then in a state of confusion and weakness, which had persisted since the 1911 revolution, and was vulnerable to pressures from the West, the newly-established Communist regime in Russia, and Japan. Several Western powers had acquired concessions in China and were interested in preserving those concessions, and therefore in seeing that China remained under a weak government, but they were also interested in promoting stability in the Far East. The Soviet Union was endeavouring to establish control over its Far Eastern territories, but, in pursuit of the long-term project of expanding Communism into Asia, was anxious to cultivate China's goodwill by assisting her to resist pressures from the Western powers and Japan. Japan had become the strong power of Asia and had improved her position by acquiring former German concessions in China and former German bases in the Pacific as a reward for her support to the Allies.

Japan however did not make use of her scope for military expansion in the Far East until 1931. For many years she accepted limitations on the development of her military power to which she had assented in the 1922 Washington Treaties, and during this interval China gained some strength and stability. This was achieved as a result of the support which the Kuomintang, the political organisation of the Chinese Nationalist movement, had decided to accept from the Soviet Union in 1923. Soviet assistance had transformed the Kuomintang into a disciplined and vigorous organisation with an effective military arm. By 1927 the Kuomintang had been able to set up a national government at Nanking, after establishing its authority over large areas of China which had been administered by local warlords. But about this time the Kuomintang ended most of its collaboration with the USSR because of resentment at Soviet sponsorship of revolutionary activities by the Chinese Communist Party, which had been founded in 1922, and which, while on the whole co-operating with the Kuomintang, was also endeavouring to supplant it.

The Japanese attack in 1931 was directed against Manchuria. As the Japanese advanced into that part of China the Soviet Union avoided challenging them, and sold to the Japanese Government its shares in the Chinese Eastern Railway, which it had inherited from the Tsarist regime and which it had retained after beginning co-operation with the Kuomintang in 1923. As the Japanese invasion continued, however, the Soviet Union saw a threat to its own territories in the Far East and began to support China. This support increased after Japan began a full-scale war against China in 1937, and Soviet forces clashed with the Japanese at points along the Sino-Soviet border, but these incidents ceased in 1939 when the USSR concluded a non-aggression pact with Nazi Germany.

A pact between Italy, Germany and Japan in September 1940 prepared the way for a Soviet-Japanese neutrality pact in April 1941, which ended Soviet support for China in her struggle against Japan. The Soviet Union continued to observe its neutrality pact with Japan after Germany's attack on the USSR in June 1941, and this gave Japan security in the north when she began a conquest of South-East Asia in December of that year. The discontinuation of Soviet support facilitated additional Japanese advances in China and evidently strained the loyalties of the Chinese Communist Party. But Mao Tse-tung, who had become leader of the Party in 1935, defended the Soviet strategy. Meanwhile, that Party was able to improve its position by co-operating with the Kuomintang in the struggle against the Japanese and in particular by building up *de facto* control in areas where its forces were operating.

The Soviet Union did not enter the war against Japan until that country was on the point of collapse, and the circumstances of its entry were unfavourable to the Kuomintang government. In February 1945, under the Yalta agreement, the USSR accepted a US invitation to attack Japan, on the following conditions:

1. The *status quo* in Outer Mongolia was to be preserved (i.e., this area was to remain a Soviet satellite).
2. Soviet "former rights" violated by Japan in 1904 were to be restored, viz.:
   (a) Southern Sakhalin and adjacent islands to be returned to the USSR.
   (b) The commercial port of Dairen to be internationalised, the "pre-eminent interests" of the Soviet Union in the port being safeguarded, and the lease of Port Arthur as a Soviet naval base to be restored.
   (c) The Chinese Eastern Railroad and the South Manchurian Railroad to be under joint Soviet-Chinese control, the "pre-eminent interests" of the USSR being safeguarded but China retaining full sovereignty in Manchuria.
3. The Kurile Islands were to be handed over to the Soviet Union.

The United States undertook to obtain China's concurrence with the conditions affecting her in the Yalta agreement, which for some time were not divulged to her, and in August 1945 those conditions were embodied in a Sino-Soviet Treaty of Friendship and Alliance which China accepted under Western pressure. But shortly before the Treaty was concluded Soviet forces entered Manchuria in order to expel the Japanese, and later while in occupation of the region those forces impeded the entry of Chinese government troops and assisted penetration of the area by Chinese Communist formations. The Chinese Communists were thus able to assume an advantageous position before they began a full scale war against the Kuomintang in 1947, but for reasons which are still not apparent the Soviet forces removed or destroyed much industrial equipment in Manchuria before withdrawing.

The course of the Communist struggle against the Kuomintang

after the defeat of Japan has been the subject of much exhaustive analysis. Notwithstanding the USA's lack of wisdom in attempting to promote co-operation between the Kuomintang and the Communists, and withholding of US military aid from the Chinese Nationalist government after 1946, it is clear that the basic reason for the collapse of the Kuomintang was its lack of public support, due to its extreme disunity and corruption.

By the third quarter of 1949 the Communists were in control of most of the country. When they set up their central government in Peking on 1 October 1949 much of the population seemed ready to co-operate with them, in the hope that their administration would prove stable and efficient.

Internal Development

The new Chinese government at first seemed to represent a somewhat mild form of Communism: it was described as a "New Democracy," because it enlisted the collaboration of that section of the middle class which had not been linked with foreign "capitalists." It soon became apparent however that the Chinese Communist authorities intended to order their regime more and more along established Communist lines. Forceful measures were introduced to consolidate control over the countryside: a ruthless campaign was conducted against "landlords" and those considered to be in sympathy with them. In 1951 a national drive against "counter-revolutionaries" resulted in the elimination of some two million people. Meanwhile an extensive public security organisation was established and an all-embracing indoctrination system was set up, to function in offices, factories, shops, etc., as well as among the population generally on a basis of residential groupings.

In 1953 the period of "New Democracy" ended and China entered the stage of *transition to socialism*: the first Five-Year Plan began. During this transition industry and agriculture were to be completely socialized and greatly developed, while that section of the former middle class which was co-operating with the regime was to undergo "ideological remoulding" so as to move into full support for the Chinese Communist Party. Meanwhile, China's culture was also to be "remoulded." Repressive

4

measures against the Christian, Islamic and Buddhist minorities, which had been introduced in 1950, were increased.

The socialization of agriculture proceeded with a rapid induction of peasants into agricultural co-operatives in 1954. A system of "reform through labour" was introduced, in order to provide more effective ideological "remoulding," in both rural and urban areas, and apparently also to supply a labour force for construction projects. Increased efforts were made to impose ideological conformity on the non-Communist intelligentsia and the public security organisation was further extended.

The pace of agricultural collectivisation was accelerated in late 1955, and by this time almost all of the small-scale industrial and commercial enterprises were under state control. In 1956 the pressures on the non-Communist intelligentsia were relaxed, but later in the year, after the unrest in Eastern Europe, the authorities evidently became very apprehensive about the extent of popular dissatisfaction within their regime.

In 1957 unrestricted expressions of popular criticism were encouraged from about mid-April to mid-June, after which the Party suddenly organised public condemnation of the critics, especially those who had voiced strong opposition to its authority. This whole operation was referred to as a Rectification Campaign and it continued until after the end of the year; the critics were denounced as "rightists." A speech by Mao Tse-tung on "contradictions," published in June, indicated that the only criticisms that the regime was prepared to accept were those which could be regarded as constructive in the context of strengthening its controls; other criticisms were to be elicited mainly in order to identify sources of opposition.

When the Rectification Campaign ended early in 1958 the second Five-Year Plan was beginning and the authorities called for accelerated progress in all fields of the economy—a "Great Leap Forward." Rapid although uneven rates of advance then developed in industry, and there was a substantial increase in agricultural production. Later in 1958 almost all the agricultural co-operatives were rapidly merged into "communes," which were intended to mobilize the rural labour force more effectively.

The communes were a notable departure from the Soviet

5

pattern of collectivization, but the Chinese claimed that these organizations were bringing China close to "Communism." As will be noted in later chapters, this caused some embarrassment to the USSR, but the Chinese continued to build up their communes, and they declared that these organisations represented a correct application of Communist theory to Chinese conditions, and were, moreover, an example to be noted in other countries. Mao Tse-tung had been closely associated with the establishment of the communes, and he was exalted as a national focus of ideological loyalties.

Foreign Affairs

The manifestation of national ambitions within Chinese Communism was a development which had been expected since the foundation of the new regime and it had important implications for China's external affairs. With the formation of the Communist government China had again become a strong power in the Far East after nearly a century of internal weakness and of humiliation and encroachment by foreign powers. She was in a position to assume again the cultural and political primacy in Asia which she had previously enjoyed for many hundreds of years. This was a source of domestic strength, and it undoubtedly had a dynamic influence on the outlook of the Chinese Communist Party, notwithstanding the internationalism embodied in Communist doctrine.

In its conduct of foreign relations, the Chinese Communist government at first co-operated closely with the USSR for the promotion of international Communism, and for the defeat of the Western "imperialist" powers. But it also entered into rivalry with the USSR, showing ambitions to extend its own power and influence in the discharge of its obligations to the various Communist movements in South and South-East Asia.

An alliance concluded with the USSR in 1950 greatly strengthened China's position in Asia at a time when Japan was still under Allied occupation and when several newly-independent South and South-East Asian countries were endeavouring to consolidate their freedom. Participation in the Korean War against modern Western forces increased respect for and fear of China in Asia, contributing to the development of neutral foreign policies by several South and South-East Asian states. These states were apprehensive about China's future intentions but on account of their hostility to colonialism were reluctant to co-operate with the Western "imperial" powers, and in particular did not wish to become involved in the question of US protection to' the Kuomintang government on Taiwan. This government had sought refuge on Taiwan following its defeat on the mainland in 1949, and after the outbreak of the Korean War had been promised US military support in the event of a Chinese Communist attack.

The South and South-East Asian countries which were developing neutral foreign policies were disposed to seek China's goodwill, but for some years the Chinese Communist government did not reciprocate. Instead, China openly encouraged revolutionary action by the Communist movements in South and South-East Asia, in line with the strategy of armed revolt in this part of Asia which had been called for by the Cominform in 1947.

In 1954, however, China began to seek the goodwill of the South and South-East Asian governments, advancing the slogan of "peaceful co-existence." By this time it was evident that the armed struggles of the various Asian Communist movements were proving unsuccessful, except in Indochina.

China exchanged pledges of "peaceful co-existence" with India and Burma during 1954, and cordial relations in a similar atmosphere were later built up with Indonesia, Ceylon and Cambodia. An immediate reason for seeking the goodwill of those countries was to discourage them from supporting the South-East Asian Collective Defence Treaty which the USA, Britain and France sponsored in September 1954. China's diplomacy contributed to the development of strong Indian opposition to the Treaty, as a result of which all the Colombo Powers except Pakistan abstained from membership.

Between 1955 and 1958 China appeared to gain increased recognition of her power and influence in Asia, through accomplished diplomacy by Premier Chou En-lai, especially during an Asian tour early in 1957. She made extensive use of "popular diplomacy" towards other Asian countries, and her sustained hostility to the West served to deter neutral Asian countries from courses of action unfavourable to her interests.

But China exercised pressures against India, the leading neutral country, during 1959, through resentment at Indian sympathies with a revolt in Tibet. This tended to compromise the whole strategy of peaceful co-existence, and it produced confusion in the Indian Communist Party, yet fear of China increased among several of her neighbours in continental South-East Asia. Indonesia however provoked China later in 1959 by discrimination against Chinese traders in rural areas of West Java, and the Chinese Communist news services showed much hostility. This could have resulted in a serious loss of prestige for China, but the Indonesian government, although persevering with its anti-Chinese measures, seemed anxious to avoid further strain in its relations with the Chinese Communist regime.

Meanwhile, although China was developing into a powerful industrial state with a strong war potential, especially as a result of rapid progress since 1958, she began to move into a somewhat isolated position in Asia during 1960 because of an open dispute with the USSR. China called for a more aggressive strategy in the promotion of International Communism, but the USSR appeared to favour a cautious approach, especially because of a desire to avoid nuclear warfare with the West. The issue appeared to be complicated, among other things, by rivalry between the two leading Communist powers for influence over the revolutionary movements elsewhere in Asia.

CHAPTER 2

State of the Nation

China presents the appearance of a totalitarian state which is rapidly developing into a major world power. Its consolidation has been accomplished with relatively less repression than that which occurred in the USSR under Stalin, and with fewer cleavages within the ruling Party, but in recent years the Chinese regime has assumed a more oppressive character.

The Chinese Communist system demands and receives much intense dedication, especially among the cadres of the Party. Although there is evidently much discontent in rural areas the atmosphere in the towns and cities appears to be one of strong solidarity with the Party and militant commitment to the expansion of Communism abroad.

The rapid development of her economy is placing China well ahead of the other underdeveloped countries in Asia, although as an industrial power she still falls behind Japan, and plays a much smaller role than Japan in world trade. But meanwhile China has been spending much more than any other Asian country on the development of her armed forces, and this, together with the receipt of Soviet equipment, has given her already a heavy superiority in conventional arms over her neighbours.

Politics

The Chinese Communist system of government became established as a highly centralised unitary structure under the 1954 constitution, and this has been retained with few modifications. The executive is the State Council, headed by the Premier; formal legislative authority is vested in the National People's Congress, but as this body meets only once a year, and then for only a few weeks, most legislation is handled by its Standing

9

Committee. The Head of State, who is known as the Chairman of the Chinese People's Republic, exercises a strong supervisory role over the activities of the executive but does not have any immediate official contact with the State Council or the Standing Committee of the National People's Congress. He may however at any time assume a direct role in day-to-day governmental affairs by convening a Supreme State Conference, over which he presides *ex officio*.

The operation of the machinery of government appears to depend largely on the positions of governmental leaders in the Chinese Communist Party: Mao Tse-tung when Head of State until early 1959 gave that office much importance, but since then his role simply as leader of the Party has overshadowed that of Liu Shao-chi as Head of State. The State Council, comprising the heads of all the Ministries, who are mostly senior members of the Party, represents a much stronger concentration of political power than the Standing Committee of the National People's Congress. Premier Chou En-lai, who chairs the State Council, has been head of the executive since 1949.

Foreign relations are handled by the Premier and the Minister of Foreign Affairs. Chou En-lai held the foreign affairs portfolio concurrently from 1949 until early 1958, when he handed it over to Chen Yi. Chou En-lai however continues to play a prominent role in the handling of foreign relations, and Chen Yi's participation in major foreign policy decisions is probably somewhat restricted, since he is not a member of the Standing Committee of the Party's Political Bureau, to which Chou En-lai belongs. This Standing Committee, which is the highest organ of the Party, does however include the Defence Minister, Lin Piao, and this presumably results in a further limitation on Chen Yi's role in foreign affairs.

No clear separation has become apparent between governmental and Party functions in China. The Party organisation parallels the machinery of government at all levels, and supplies much impetus to the administration, but it also plays a direct role in many social, economic and legal affairs. This has been illustrated especially by the establishment, in early 1961, of regional bureaux for the Party's Central Committee, covering the areas which were controlled by regional governmental authorities during the first few years of the regime. There has been no suggestion that the regional governmental authorities might be re-established, but it has been obvious that the new regional Party bureaux will have an important administrative role, notably in strengthening the management of the communes.[1]

The greater part of the work of the government concerns the administration of the economy, and in this field direct Party activity has become very much greater since 1958. In order to produce a "Great Leap Forward" in the economy the Party has exerted strong pressures on management, workers and peasants, and it has carried on a campaign against those who have criticized the economic value of this drive. The critics, who have evidently been persons in the management levels, have been condemned for "rightist" thinking, and the campaign has produced an atmosphere in which demands from the Party for continually higher increases in output cannot be questioned. There had been evidence of resentment towards the Party among administrative officials, but the Party had reiterated that its leadership in the management of the economy was absolutely necessary for rapid progress.[2]

After the 1957 Rectification Campaign, presumably as a result of increased anxieties by the authorities about the danger of popular unrest, the Party also increased its role in public indoctrination and social mobilisation. Meanwhile, by operating a system of periodic manual labour in rural areas for government officials and its own cadres, the Party increased and strengthened its supervisory role in relation to the administration.

Behind the increased activities of the Party there appears to be faith in its organisation as a more effective means of eliciting public co-operation than the State apparatus, which is evidently regarded as being prone to "bureaucratism." Some sacrifice of managerial efficiency is accepted, but in the economy as a whole progress is intended to be achieved in waves. That is, periods of rapid but uneven advancement are meant to be followed by

1 NCNA, 20 January 1961.
2 Liao Kao-lung, On Political Leadership, *People's Daily*, Peking, 5 December 1959.

11

stages of consolidation in which the imbalances and dislocations of hasty development are overcome.

The fall-off in public co-operation with the regime which became noticeable in 1957 appears to have continued. During the Rectification Campaign of that year it had become evident that there was much opposition to the Chinese Communist Party's monopoly of political power and to the sacrifices which it was demanding. This opposition was present among the industrial workers, the non-Communist "intellectuals," the peasants and even in some sections of the Party.[3] Since the Rectification Campaign, the Party has employed more drastic measures for indoctrination and social mobilisation, especially through the commune system; the austerities have continued; and the efforts demanded from the workers and the peasants have increased.

In rural areas discontent became more extensive because of a serious food shortage due to natural calamities in 1959 and 1960. A communique issued by the Chinese Communist Party's Central Committee in January 1961 indicated that a significant proportion of the urban and rural populations were not supporting the authorities, that sabotage was being carried out in the communes and that some disorders were occurring in the villages and the cities: "a few" officials were wavering in their support for the government.[4] This disaffection would no doubt have been less if there had been no food shortage, but it is likely that some of that shortage resulted from, as well as contributing to, the discontent in the communes.

Although there have been some indications of cleavages within the Chinese Communist Party in connection with the harsh social and economic policies followed since 1958, the Party as a whole has maintained an appearance of unity. Some cleavages may have preceded the decision in December 1958 that Mao Tse-tung would not continue as Head of State, but after he relinquished this office a movement began to build up his stature as the leader of the Party, and this became quite pronounced in 1960. Since Liu Shao-chi became Head of State the question of succession to Mao Tse-tung, which had previously seemed likely

3 Report by Teng Hsiao-ping, Party Secretary-General, NCNA, 18 October 1957.
4 NCNA, 20 January 1961.

to promote dissension, appears to have been resolved in advance. As a public figure, however, Liu Shao-chi has been overshadowed by Mao Tse-tung and his stature is considerably less than that of Chou En-lai, who, especially through his handling of foreign affairs, has enjoyed prominence second only to that of the Party leader.

The Party's campaign against "rightist" elements who were not supporting the drive for rapid economic development involved censure of certain unidentified individuals in the upper levels of its own organisation. In the course of this campaign, Vice-Premier Ch'en Yun, a Politburo member with much experience in the regime's economic administration, disappeared from public life. In the lower levels of the Party, especially in rural areas, a purge seemed likely to develop out of a new "Rectification Campaign" announced early in 1961 for the strengthening of Party control in the communes.[5]

Society and Culture

The Chinese Communist regime is endeavouring to "remould" Chinese society, using psychological pressures much stronger than those which have been applied in the USSR. Mass indoctrination is intended to remove all former familial, religious and economic loyalties and to build up wholehearted dedication to the Communist Party. The class structure has been altered by the elimination of "landlords" and the upper middle class; by the transformation of the middle and lower middle classes into State employees; and by the collectivisation of the peasantry. In theory the Chinese Communist Party is a movement operating among the workers and peasants, and therefore Party functionaries do not officially form a separate class, but the members of the Party organisation and the officials of the administration do constitute a separate social grouping *de facto* and are certainly regarded as such by the bulk of the population. Party documents frequently imply recognition of a clear-cut distinction between the authorities and the masses of the people. There is often stress on the importance of strengthening ties between the Party

5 Announced in connection with the establishment of the Regional Party Bureaux mentioned above—NCNA, 20 January 1961.

and government on the one hand and the general population on the other.

The workers, peasants, and those sections of the former middle class who are being "remoulded" constitute "the people." Outside the ranks of "the people" are the "counter-revolutionary" elements, who oppose the regime. There is a constant search for "counter-revolutionaries" and after seizure they are executed or obliged to undergo "corrective" labour and indoctrination. Among the various social classes who make up the "people" there are many individuals whose outlook is still "bourgeois," and the official view is that these are likely to become "counter-revolutionaries" unless they undergo "reform."

For doctrinaire reasons, the regime regards the urban workers as a more advanced class than the peasants, and it ensures that living standards for those workers are higher than in the countryside. Peasants have endeavoured to migrate into the cities, but this has been opposed by the authorities, and surplus urban labour has been sent to rural areas.

The long-term intention is to break down the distinction between workers and peasants by transforming the latter into operatives on mechanised farms and extending the commune system into urban areas, but for the present the pace of mechanisation in agriculture is restricted, since the investment priority of this branch of the economy remains low.

The establishment of the new class structure has been accompanied by the destruction of traditional group loyalties. The "extended family" system has been broken down, with much emphasis on the "emancipation" of women, and clan loyalties have been weakened in the process of socialisation and indoctrination, and through the purge of "counter-revolutionaries." In recent years, the inauguration of the communes has meant a further breaking of family ties, since husbands and wives have been allocated to separate work teams and children have been placed in the communal nurseries. All are thus expected to transfer their loyalties to the "big family" of the commune, and one of the advantages of this is that the indoctrination of the children will be more effective.[6]

6 *China Youth*, 1 May 1960; see also editions of 1 June and 16 July 1960.

In the cultural life of the nation, the Chinese Communist Party has continued to consolidate its "leadership." In place of Confucianism, Taoism, the old cults of animism and ancestor-worship, and the religions of Christianity, Mohammedanism and Buddhism, the Party has endeavoured to impose dialectical and historical materialism, and hence a militant dedication to the building up of Communism in China and throughout the world. Among the various religious influences, the resistance of Christianity to this "remoulding" appears to have been the most active, and the regime's hostility to Christianity, although concealed by a facade of tolerance, has been extremely virulent.

The basic Confucian ideal of social harmony has been opposed by a doctrine of incessant "struggle" against "bourgeois" and "counter-revolutionary" influences. In place of the goodwill which formerly contributed to social harmony, the pervasive and unending "struggles" produce widespread divisions among the people, for each is from time to time under pressure to indict some of the others. The divisive effects of the "struggles" enable the Party to consolidate its political controls, since it is difficult for potential opponents to unite, and this in turn contributes to the effectiveness of the Party's cultural "remoulding."

Emphasis on the indoctrination of the young has been increased since 1957.[7] Access to higher education has become more conditional on a record of strong loyalty to the regime. Such loyalty must be shown especially in a willingness to face assignments to rural labour, and the experience of this gives a strong incentive to acquire higher status.

The process of cultural "remoulding" has been most evident in literature. The Party has called for a continuous flow of "socialist" writing and has prevented the circulation of "bourgeois" works. The need for popular appeal in the "socialist" literature has been recognised, but the requirement for indoctrination has remained heavy, and as a result works produced under the regime have in most cases been dull. The prohibition against reflecting "bourgeois" values is very strong, and this category is a broad one, for the projection of any aesthetic quality unrelated to the class struggle can be condemned under this heading. There is no

[7] See article by Education Minister in *People's Daily*, Peking, 8 October 1959.

"middle way" which an author may follow between "socialist" and "bourgeois" writing.

The demand for popular appeal in literature, however, and the restlessness of literary circles under the restrictions of Party control, have caused limited departures from "socialist" standards and these have been condemned as "revisionism." A new drive to eliminate "revisionism" in literature began in 1960.[8]

In the sciences, although there has been much insistence on political control, the Party has proceeded more cautiously, recognising some need for free discussion and noting that doctrine cannot substitute for research.[9] The Party is however sensitive to the danger of implied criticisms of its dialectical materialism arising out of advances in the sciences. More importantly, the Party is opposed to the development among scientists of an exclusive preoccupation with their work, since that will involve neglect of "politics." What is called for is a combination of professional competence and strong loyalty to the Communist system.

The extent to which political control has furthered or hindered scientific progress in the regime is difficult to assess. There has been much pressure for quick results in scientific research to meet the needs of the industrialisation programme. The general level of scientific development however has probably remained low owing to the shortage of experienced personnel, the distractions of political interference, and isolation from foreign scientific developments.

Economy

The Chinese Communist government is continuing its efforts to build up an independent, industrialised, highly self-sufficient economy, on a "socialist" basis, with a substantial war potential. To finance industrialisation, a relatively large volume of agricultural produce is procured by the regime for export and to meet the needs of the expanding urban areas; living standards are kept low in the countryside, but little finance is made available for

8 See *Literature and Art News*, No. 1, of 1960, and article on "Neutralist Thinking" in *Kwangming Daily*, 13 November 1960.
9 *Red Flag*, 1 March 1961.

agricultural development, which is intended to proceed on a labour-intensive basis. A high proportion of the industrial output is reinvested in industry.[10]

This development policy has become heavily dependent on the efficiency of the communes in expanding agricultural production and restricting the living standards of the peasants. The drastic regimentation of those organisations, however, including their disruption of family ties, may be proving counter-productive. Some restoration of individual freedom to the peasants in the communes occurred early in 1961, when private side-line agricultural pursuits were encouraged and restricted markets were set up for local products. These measures however were evidently intended to last only until the severe food shortage had been overcome.

The investment priority accorded to industry—mainly heavy industry—has been reflected in budget figures since 1954, and, together with the recent intensified pressures for higher production, it has led to notable advances in industrial output. Capital construction for heavy and light industry averaged about 50% of state expenditure between 1954 and 1958, compared with an average of about 11% for agriculture, forestry and water conservation. Steel production rose from 1.77 million tons in 1953 to 5.35 million tons in 1957 and 13.35 million tons in 1959. Between 1953 and 1959 coal production increased about five times, reaching 347.8 million tons, while electric power production also increased almost five times, reaching 41,500 million Kwh. Heavy increases were registered in the output of machine tools, electric motors, power generators, locomotives and motor vehicles, but only moderate advances were made in the production of cotton, paper, cigarettes, vegetable oil, sugar, salt and other consumer goods.[11]

During 1960 heavy industrial production made further progress, but the rate of development in 1961 was to be slower because of the setbacks in agriculture during 1959 and 1960, which reduced the amount of primary produce available for

10 See W. W. Rostow, *The Prospects for Communist China*, Massachusetts Institute of Technology, 1954, p. 303.
11 See table based on NCNA releases in *Far Eastern Economic Review*, 29 September 1960, p. 731.

export. Grain production had risen from about 166 million tons in 1953 to 275 million tons in 1959.

The accelerated progress in industry and agriculture since 1958 has been achieved mainly by intense political pressures for higher outputs, with little use of material rewards. In industry the pressures for higher production evidently resulted in some lowering of standards, because improvements in the quality of industrial products were called for in February 1961. In particular it appeared that the regime was dissatisfied with the quality of the products from the small local industrial enterprises which had been set up in large numbers during 1958.[12]

The advances in heavy industrial development have further enlarged China's war potential. No armaments industry has been identified as such, but the Second Ministry of Machine Industry is believed to be responsible for military production, and allocations for it have presumably been included in the budget item for heavy industry. Defence expenditure, which is a separate armed forces apart from the provision of equipment by the item in the budget, may have comprised sums spent on the Second Ministry of Machine Industry. Some of the payments for military equipment received from the USSR also may not be covered under the heading of defence expenditure, for repayments of foreign loans constitute another section in the budget, and there is some evidence that Soviet military equipment for the armed forces has been obtained on a loan basis.[13]

The defence allocation in both 1959 and 1960 was Y5800 million—about US $2300 million. Defence spending has been running at about this level since 1954 and it has usually been greater than the amount allocated for investment in agriculture; in the 1960 budget, investments in the communes and in capital construction for agriculture, forestry, water conservation and the meteorological service amount to Y5410 million.

The level of defence spending in the Chinese regime is considerably greater than what the Soviet Union's was at a comparable stage of development.[14] China has acquired heavy

12 Statement by Po I-po, Chairman of the National Economic Commission, NCNA, 4 February 1961.

13 *Moscow-Peking Axis,* Council on Foreign Relations, New York, 1957, p. 90.

14 W. W. Rostow, *The Prospects for Communist China,* p. 322.

military superiority over her Asian neighbours, although so far she has apparently not begun production of nuclear weapons. This military superiority will probably be much greater by the late 1960s, since defence spending in all other Asian states is likely to remain far below the level in China.

Meanwhile China's economic development is being accompanied by an expansion of her role in international trade. Although official Chinese figures are not available, it appears from information supplied by partner countries that China's foreign commerce has been about half that of Japan over the past few years and that her exports have been somewhat higher than those of India. China's total exports in 1956-8 averaged more than US $1500 million annually, and of these approximately half were sent each year to the USSR while almost 25% went to Eastern Europe.[15] In recent years there have evidently been substantial increases in China's foreign trade, but the preference for other Communist countries has continued, although there have been notable increases in imports from Western Europe.

In Asian trade, China's position appears to have undergone little change. In 1956-58 exports to other Asian countries were on the average less than half of the Japanese level of about US $1000 million and her imports from those countries were less than a third of the Japanese average, which was about US $800 million; meanwhile although China's exports to other Asian countries were about double those of India, India's imports from Asia were very much higher than China's.

The direction in which her economy is developing implies only a gradual expansion of China's position in Asian trade. China's demand for primary products from South and South-East Asia is increasing at a slow rate, and her emphasis on heavy industrial development implies only limited increases in her exports of light industrial products. China cannot export capital goods in significant quantities, but she is making an additional impact on Asian economic relations by providing aid for development to the smaller neutral countries.

15 U.N. Statistical Papers, Series T, Vol. X, No. 8, *Direction of International Trade.*

CHAPTER 3

Foreign Relations Record

When the Chinese Communist government was founded on 1 October 1949 its announced intentions in foreign affairs were to

(a) protect China's independence, freedom, and integrity
(b) work for lasting international peace and friendly co-operation between all countries
(c) establish cordial relations with foreign governments whose attitudes were friendly
(d) unite with the Soviet Union and other Communist states and movements in the struggle against the "imperialists," and in particular the USA
(e) protect the rights and interests of the Overseas Chinese.[1]

The first point meant that the regime's authority had to be extended into those parts of China which were still under Nationalist control, but the Chinese Communist leaders also apparently had in mind the recovery of authority over areas which had become detached from "China" in the past and which the Nationalists had not regained. Later it became clear that the Communist authorities were thinking in particular of Tibet, of certain border territories controlled by India and Burma, and possibly also of Mongolia and Korea. Whether the Chinese also had in mind absorption of South-East Asia as an area of former Chinese suzerainty is not clear, but it did become evident that they hoped to develop strong influence in this region by encouragement and support of the local Communist movements.

The promotion of lasting international peace had a special significance in the Chinese Communist outlook. Permanent international peace was considered possible only with the

1 See Common Programme of the Chinese Peoples Political Consultative Conference, NCNA, 29 September 1949; and Mao Tse-tung's pronouncement of 1 July 1949 *On the Peoples Democratic Dictatorship*.

elimination of "imperialism" and the establishment of world communism, and the achievement of that peace necessitated wars against the "imperialists." This theme had been stressed in Mao Tse-tung's writings before the establishment of Communism in China, and it was to be put forward very forcibly in 1960.[2]

The principle of developing cordiality with countries other than the "imperialist" ones reflected a desire to gain temporary allies among the non-Communist countries and thus help to isolate the "main enemy"—the leading "imperialist" powers. In accordance with this principle, the Chinese Communist government responded in 1949-50 to official recognition by India, Pakistan, Ceylon and Burma, as well as by Egypt, Syria, Yemen, Denmark, Holland, Finland, Norway, Sweden and Switzerland, and took the initiative in establishing official relations with Indonesia; but treated coldly a British gesture of recognition, regarding this as merely a step towards negotiating the opening of diplomatic relations with the British government. Yet, although the way was open for China to build up cordial relations with several neighbouring countries, she showed considerable disdain towards the non-Communist Asian governments, which she regarded as "bourgeois" instruments of "imperialist" control: China's sympathies lay with the various Asian Communist movements which had begun or were preparing for armed insurrections. In November 1949 the Chinese Communist Party had exhorted those movements to follow China's example. That was done at an Asian and Australasian Trade Union Conference in Peking, where the present Head of State, Liu Shao-chi, declared that the people in "colonial and semi-colonial" countries should take the Chinese path in order to achieve "independence" and "peoples democracy": this was mainly a path of "armed struggle" by "liberation armies" under Communist leadership.[3] At this time, in response to exhortations by the Soviet Union, the Malayan, Burmese and Filippino Communist Parties were in armed revolt, and the Vietnamese Communist Party was leading a popular struggle against French rule

---

2 See article by Fu Chung, *People's Daily*, Peking, 6 and 7 October 1960.

3 NCNA, 16 November 1949; see Captain M. Kennedy, *A History of Communism in East Asia*, Frederick A. Praeger, New York, 1957, p. 380; and J. H. Brimmell, *Communism In South-East Asia*, Oxford University Press, 1959, p. 259.

in Indochina; but insurgent activities by the Indian Communist Party were proving unsuccessful and a resort to violence by the Indonesian Communist Party had been crushed.

The principle of alliance with the USSR had been expounded in Mao-Tse-tung's writings before October 1949. The Chinese Communist regime would side with the USSR against "imperialism" and there could be no question of a "middle way."[4] The Chinese Communist Party believed that Communist struggles in individual countries required support from other Communist states and movements, and that the activities of all such states and movements should be unified under Soviet leadership.

Under a Treaty of Alliance, Friendship and Mutual Assistance announced on 14 February 1950, China was promised Soviet economic and military aid, and each side pledged co-operation with the other in foreign affairs, and common action in the event of aggression by "Japan or any state allied with Japan." Separate notes in effect sanctioned Mongolia's continuation as a Soviet satellite, but arrangements were made to terminate Soviet use of Port Arthur naval base and of the Chinese Changchung railway. Soviet economic aid worth US $300 million was pledged over a five-year period.[5]

After conclusion of the Sino-Soviet alliance, close co-operation between the two regimes was apparent in their diplomacy and external propaganda, while within China Soviet achievements were popularised and the people were exhorted to "learn" from the Soviet example. The cult of Stalin as a great leader also developed in China. Meanwhile the USSR gave support to the Chinese Communist government in its diplomacy towards the non-Communist countries. The Chinese Communist government on 8 January 1950 formally claimed representation in the United Nations in place of Nationalist China, and this demand was backed by the USSR, but the move was unsuccessful and the Soviet Union, in protest, withdrew its representatives from the UN. This Soviet boycott was still in force when the Korean War began.

The Chinese Communist government's concern for the Over-

---

4 See especially Mao Tse-tung, *On the Peoples Democratic Dictatorship*, 1 July 1949.
5 Details of these agreements are given in Chapter 6.

seas Chinese reflected an interest in establishing political controls over the Chinese minorities in South-East Asia. This proceeded with little hindrance in the countries which opened diplomatic relations with the new Chinese regime, for example, in Indonesia and Burma, and, later, in Cambodia, but progressed slowly in countries which had avoided official links with the Chinese Communist authorities, such as Thailand and the Philippines.

As might have been anticipated, the principle of alignment with the USSR in the promotion of international Communism soon became evident as the dominant factor in China's foreign policy. But within a few years it became clear that China's national interests were also exerting much influence on the regime's foreign relations. Ideological commitment and national interests were apparent when China participated in the Korean War.

Korean War

The Chinese Communist government gave moral support to the North Korean attack against South Korea in June 1950 and reacted sharply to the intervention by UN forces in Korea. The US decision to protect the Chinese Nationalist Government on Taiwan was denounced as "aggression" against China and interference in her internal affairs. The Chinese Communist authorities claimed that the UN (principally US) intervention in Korea was also motivated by aggressive designs against China, and they stressed this in news comments and diplomacy directed towards the newly independent Asian countries, especially India.

The Chinese Communist leaders however did not attempt military action against Taiwan and they evidently did not intend intervening in Korea unless the United Nations forces gained the initiative and penetrated North Korea. When the UN forces recovered ground after withdrawing into the South, notice was given that China would intervene if the UN advance continued across the 38th parallel. The Chinese, however, waited until the UN forces had reached parts of the Manchurian border before committing their own troops, in November 1950, and even then the intervention was cautious. The Chinese accepted a UN

Security Council invitation to discuss the matter at Lake Success, although demanding that their complaint against US protection of the Chinese Nationalists should also be considered. The USA, France and Britain endeavoured to assure the Chinese Communist government that the UN forces in Korea would respect the Chinese frontier with Korea, but those forces meanwhile continued to advance towards other parts of the frontier and the Chinese then took the offensive.[6]

After forcing a UN retreat into South Korea the Chinese and North Korean armies were in turn obliged to fall back towards the 38th parallel. A cease-fire was proposed by the Soviet representative at the UN in June 1951, but when talks began with the UN command the Chinese opposed the principle of voluntary POW repatriation which was put forward by the UN. The Chinese Communists stood to lose face from this principle because the UN forces held many Chinese prisoners who did not desire repatriation. The Chinese Communist-North Korean command did not compromise on this question until July 1953, when they accepted a cease-fire along a line which curved across the 38th parallel.

An extension and some consolidation of Chinese Communist authority had meanwhile been achieved in Tibet. The country had been invaded by Chinese Communist forces in late 1950. Indian efforts to mediate on behalf of the Tibetans were rebuffed; the Chinese claimed that the matter was entirely domestic, and their firmness discouraged Indian opposition. Chinese control of Tibet was formalised under an agreement of 23 May 1951 with the Tibetan "local government" which promised Tibet "regional autonomy" under the overall authority of the central government in Peking, and which stipulated that the Tibetan government would voluntarily carry out "reforms," although promising that the central government would not impose changes in the Tibetan political system. The Tibetan government acknowledged that in the past it had taken an "unpatriotic" attitude towards the Motherland.[7]

6 See *Survey of International Affairs 1949-50*, Royal Institute of International Affairs, p. 489.
7 NCNA, 23 May 1951. The version given in *Documents on International Affairs, 1951*, by the Royal Institute of International Affairs, is abbreviated.

Indochina

After the cease-fire in Korea there was heavy emphasis on China's economic development, and China asserted her desire for a peaceful international environment, but she increased her logistic support to the Communist-led nationalist movement, the Viet Minh, in Indochina. This support had developed after communications across Kwangsi had been improved and extended to the Indochina border in 1952.

Despite the flow of Chinese Communist military assistance to the Viet Minh, the French authorities in Indochina and at home were anxious not to provoke the Chinese. The French forces in Indochina had been receiving large quantities of US military equipment since 1950, but France did not wish to have direct US military assistance in Indochina except in the event of large-scale Chinese Communist intervention, and the US government also was evidently not in favour of joining the conflict unless such intervention occurred.[8] The Chinese could thus expand their logistic support to the Viet Minh without risking the security of their own regime, and with a reasonable hope of securing a French defeat by attrition.

The Viet Minh improved their overall position in 1953 and morale in France was lowered, but although the Viet Minh could now expect victory within a reasonable time they also had to give more weight to the possibility of active US support for the French, even in the absence of Chinese intervention. Hence in 1954 both the Viet Minh and the Chinese Communists apparently decided not to accept the risks of pursuing a total victory but to negotiate a settlement.

Western recognition of China's important role in Indochina facilitated her participation in the Geneva Conference which opened in April 1954. After an inconclusive consideration of the Korean problem, the Conference reached a settlement in Indochina, subsequent to a concession which promised a withdrawal of Viet Minh troops from Laos and Cambodia. The settlement provided for a cease-fire and gave control of North Vietnam to the Viet Minh; Viet Minh troops were to be withdrawn from the

8 See *Survey of International Affairs*, 1953, Royal Institute of International Affairs, p. 294.

south and that part of Vietnam was to remain under the control of the Republic of Vietnam — i.e., the Vietnamese state which had been sponsored by the French. Elections were to be held within two years for the reunification of Vietnam, and this clearly offered the Viet Minh a way to achieve eventual control of the country through gaining the upper hand in a coalition government. Meanwhile it seemed likely that *de facto* Viet Minh control could be established in the South by underground Communists, as the country was in a state of extreme confusion and the authority of the South Vietnam government appeared to be disintegrating.

Peaceful Co-existence

Through the diplomacy of Premier Chou En-lai at Geneva, the Chinese Communists increased their international prestige and secured wider credence for their dedication to "peaceful co-existence." The way had been prepared for this by an exchange of pledges of "peaceful co-existence" with India shortly before the Geneva Conference began,[9] and by a repetition of those pledges during a visit to India by Premier Chou En-lai in June 1954. Subsequently, Chinese Communist efforts to promote an atmosphere of "peaceful co-existence" in Asia were facilitated by Indian goodwill, especially as signified by Prime Minister Nehru's first visit to China during October 1954. Burmese goodwill was also of some importance for China's "peaceful co-existence" campaign; Premier U Nu exchanged pledges of "peaceful co-existence" with Premier Chou En-lai in June 1954.

The new diplomacy was intended to demonstrate China's peaceful intentions towards neighbouring states and in particular to discourage the South and South-East Asian countries from alignment with the West. After the conclusion of the Geneva Agreements, the USA, Britain and France began to sponsor a South-East Asian Collective Defence Treaty, in order to guarantee the security of South Vietnam, Cambodia and Laos, and of any South-East Asian country which might be willing to join the pact. The Chinese strongly denounced the USA for its efforts to establish this Treaty, and alleged that any Asian

[9] In connection with a Sino-Indian agreement on Tibet, NCNA, 29 April 1954.

country which joined it would be co-operating with the USA in "aggressive" plans against China. China desired peaceful co-operation with other Asian countries, and this could be secured by those countries if they avoided complicity with the USA. Premier Chou En-lai stated on 11 August 1954 that China was working for "world peace and the progress of mankind," but that this was being opposed by "aggressive circles in the United States" who were aiding the Chinese Nationalists, remilitarising Japan, and establishing an "anti-Communist military alliance" in South-East Asia; China would administer "defeat after defeat" to this aggressive policy and endeavour to expand and develop her peaceful co-operation with other nations.

At this time the Chinese Communist authorities were making a vigorous demonstration of their intention to seize Taiwan, presumably in order to make it clear that any Asian state which aligned itself with the USA would be involved with that country in "aggression" against China over an internal Chinese affair. Meanwhile China's efforts to obstruct the formation of the South-East Asian Collective Defence Treaty were made easier by the opposition which India showed towards this Treaty. India condemned the formation of the Treaty as a provocative step and her stand was largely responsible for the non-participation of Burma, Ceylon and Indonesia. These abstentions made it easier for the Chinese to extend their "peaceful co-existence" diplomacy, especially with a view to weakening the resolution of the Asian members of the Treaty: Pakistan, Thailand and the Philippines.

China participated in the Afro-Asian Conference sponsored by the Colombo Powers at Bandung in April 1955. Premier Chou En-lai strongly emphasised his regime's desire for peaceful co-operation with other Asian countries, and declared his willingness to negotiate with the USA for a relaxation of tension in the Far East. Chou En-lai's diplomacy at the Conference enhanced China's prestige in Asia, and towards the end of the Conference the Indonesian, Pakistani and Ceylonese Prime Ministers accepted invitations to visit China. After the Conference Chou En-lai made a short official visit to Djakarta, and relations with Indonesia were brought to a very cordial level. A Sino-Indonesian

Dual Nationality Agreement was signed, and it provided that the Overseas Chinese in Indonesia would choose Indonesian or Chinese Communist citizenship within two years. The agreement received wide notice, because it was the first of its kind to be concluded by the Chinese Communist government with another Asian country. The Chinese Communist government had previously indicated its desire to conclude citizenship agreements with Asian states which had Chinese minorities, and in 1954 had secured a promise from Burma that the citizenship of the Chinese in that country would be settled at the earliest opportunity.

Meanwhile the new diplomacy of "peaceful co-existence" obliged the Chinese Communist government to de-emphasise the role of the Overseas Chinese as extensions of the motherland's authority. In late 1954 the Chinese Communist government stressed its willingness to encourage the Overseas Chinese to become loyal citizens of their adopted countries, and declared its readiness to settle their nationality. Nevertheless it was still clear that the Chinese Communist authorities expected the Overseas Chinese to play a valuable role in the spread of Communism in Asia, especially by promoting "friendship" for the Communist regime.[10]

After the Afro-Asian Conference, China's prestige became further consolidated in Asia but the co-operation which she had been receiving from India began to decline. In July and August 1954 there had been Sino-Indian diplomatic exchanges over minor boundary issues, and further exchanges began in June 1955. The expansion of Chinese influence was beginning to involve rivalry with India, and to a degree this was signified by the Indian government's opposition to Chinese Communist proposals for a second Afro-Asian Conference. At the same time the Chinese Communist authorities were finding it necessary to re-appraise their policy towards India because the USSR had begun to give high priority to the cultivation of Indian goodwill. This was first made apparent during June 1955, when Prime Minister Nehru visited the Soviet Union and received more deference than had been shown to him on his first visit to China in October of

10 See A. Doak Barnett, *Communist China and Asia*, Harper & Bros., New York, 1960, p. 188.

the previous year. A hint of something similar in the Far East was given about the same time, when the USSR, responding to the formation of the Hatoyama government in Japan, began negotiations for a normalisation of relations with that country but showed little concern for China's interests in the matter.

The Soviet leaders Krushchev and Bulganin toured India, Burma and Afghanistan during November 1955, making offers of economic aid and engaging in forms of personal diplomacy which were evidently intended to emulate the successes of Chou En-lai. The two Russians supported the Indian case on the Kashmir dispute and the Afghan case on the Pushtoonistan issue, and thereby gave provocation to Pakistan, although the Chinese had been paying special attention to the cultivation of goodwill in that country: at Bandung, the Pakistani Prime Minister had accepted an invitation to visit China.

The Chinese campaign for "peaceful co-existence" was continued successfully during 1956. Prime Minister Suhrawardy of Pakistan visited China, and both the Cambodian and Laotian governments were drawn towards "peaceful co-existence" in the hope that this would lead to restraint on Viet Minh subversion within their borders. Meanwhile there were signs of a relaxation of authoritarian controls in China, and this enabled the regime to assume a somewhat liberal appearance. Later in the year, and in early 1957, when Soviet prestige had fallen as a result of the Hungarian revolt and the unrest in Poland, Chou En-lai undertook a long Asian tour in which doctrinaire considerations seemed to have been set aside in favour of making a wide popular appeal. He visited India, Burma, Pakistan, Cambodia, Nepal, Ceylon and Afghanistan.

Bloc Relations

The uncertain situations in the USSR and in the Communist movement generally after de-Stalinisation in early 1956 and the Eastern European troubles at the end of the year were exploited by the Chinese, within limits, in order to strengthen their own position in the Communist Bloc. They pronounced authoritatively on the issues raised by the denunciation of Stalin and the unrest in Eastern Europe, making it clear that in their view

Soviet leadership was to be accepted only with considerable qualifications, and that other Communist governments had to protect their own interests against possible Soviet encroachments.[11] For most of 1957 the Chinese showed reluctance to endorse Soviet authority in the international Communist movement, and, although they made a show of enthusiasm for Soviet leadership in November 1957, emphasis on their own rather independent status became evident in 1958. In that year the Chinese diverged from the Soviet pattern by introducing "communes," they showed antipathy towards the Soviet line of diplomacy on the Middle East crisis, and they manifested resentment at the lack of Soviet support for a new campaign which they were directing against Taiwan.

In October 1958 more tension developed on the Sino-Indian border, and early in 1959 the Chinese reacted in a very hostile way to Indian sympathies with a revolution in Tibet, and especially to the Indian government's decision to grant asylum to the Dalai Lama. Later in the year there were some serious border incidents, and the Chinese, who had previously been evasive about their views on the delineation of the border, formally indicated that they were claiming large areas from India east of Bhutan and in the State of Jammu and Kashmir. Moreover, the Chinese made it clear that they would not withdraw from certain areas which India regarded as being on her side of the border. During all these events, however, the Soviet attitude was neutral.

The Chinese case against India received no public support from the USSR and on the contrary the Soviet Union increased its cordiality towards India. Since 1955 the USSR had provided much economic aid to India and had built up friendly relations with the Indian government.

When Soviet Premier Krushchev visited the USA in September 1959 to prepare for a Summit meeting with the British, French and US heads of government, Chinese Communist official statements and news comments began pointed criticisms of the concept of "peaceful co-existence" with the West. The Chinese

---

11 See pronouncement *More on the Historical Experience of the Dictatorship of the Proletariat, People's Daily*, Peking, 29 December 1956.

declared that there was no real possibility of such co-existence, and that to look for it was misguided; all possible pressures had to be built up against the imperialistic Western countries in order to discourage them from "aggression." The Chinese argued this more vigorously after the unsuccessful Summit of May 1960, and were then criticised by the USSR for naive left-wing extremism; the Soviet Union demanded scope for compromises and settlements with the West.

Meanwhile a chauvinist trend developed in the evolution of Communist doctrine in China, and this was signified by the elevation of Mao Tse-tung as the sage of the nation and as the greatest theorist of the international Communist movement. The Chinese Communist authorities continued to declare solidarity with the Soviet Union, but at the same time they adhered to their more belligerent line, and encouraged a resumption of violent methods by the Asian Communist movements.[12]

The West

China's relations with the West had undergone few changes since 1950. After her intervention in the Korean War the UN called on its members to ban shipments of strategic goods to China, and the NATO powers together with Japan applied an embargo against her which was more comprehensive than one which they were maintaining against the USSR. The embargo against China continued after the end of the Korean War, but strong business interests in Western Europe and especially in Britain began pressing for its modification. This was done by stages, until in 1958 it was brought down to the level maintained against the USSR. The USA, however, continued with a complete embargo against trade with China which it had introduced during the Korean War.

China denounced the Western efforts to deny her access to strategic materials but for ideological and strategic reasons she conducted about 75% of her foreign trade with the USSR and Eastern Europe, and showed little desire to build up trade with the West in commodities which were unrestricted. Until mid-1954 the Chinese reacted coldly to British attempts at trade

12 *Red Flag*, 24th issue of 1960, NCNA, 15 December 1960.

promotion, imposing crushing burdens on British enterprises in China and gave little official status to the British diplomatic mission in Peking. The main intention behind all this appears to have been to induce Britain to exercise a modifying influence on US policy towards the Chinese Communist government.

In June 1954 the Chinese agreed to recognise the head of the British diplomatic mission in Peking as the British Chargé d'Affaires, instead of merely the British "negotiation representative," and they promised to send a Chargé d'Affaires to London. The establishment of relations at that level was completed in late 1954, but the Chinese refused to accept British representation at the Ambassadorial level because Britain regarded the status of Taiwan as indeterminate and withheld support from the Chinese Communist claim for entry into the United Nations.

The United States had avoided recognition of the Chinese Communist government in 1949 but had left certain consular officials on the mainland. The Chinese Communist government refused to accord any official status to those officials, however, and some of them, after being arrested, were expelled. The US government then became strongly opposed to any immediate recognition of the Chinese Communist regime. When the Korean War broke out in June 1950, the US government declared that it would protect Taiwan, while preventing any Nationalist attack on the mainland. After this it was clear that any US gesture to accord official recognition to the Chinese Communist government would be unacceptable in Peking, because it had been laid down firmly that foreign governments which desired official links with the Chinese regime would have to sever relations with the Chinese Nationalists and recognize Chinese Communist sovereignty over Taiwan.

US protection of Taiwan continued after the end of the Korean War but in August and September 1954 the Chinese Communists vigorously asserted their intention of seizing the island. Quemoy was bombarded, and the UN was requested to call upon the USA to withdraw its forces from Taiwan and the off-shore islands. The USA however concluded a Mutual Security pact with the Chinese Nationalist Government on 1 December

1954. This was denounced by the Chinese Communist authorities, but their successes in the diplomacy of "peaceful co-existence" were evidently counselling some demonstration of a willingness to compromise on the issues related to Taiwan. At the Afro-Asian Conference in 1955 Chou En-lai offered to negotiate with the USA for a relaxation of tensions in the Far East, and subsequently it was agreed that Sino-US ambassadorial talks would begin in Geneva on 1 August 1955. These talks, however, were to have few results. Chou En-lai did not indicate any real change of policy concerning Taiwan.[13]

During 1956 China strongly denounced the USA for supporting South Vietnam's refusal to hold national elections with North Vietnam for the reunification of the country as prescribed by the 1954 Geneva Agreement. The South Vietnam government considered that it was not bound by the Geneva Agreement because it had not signed it. The Chinese, however, although they accused the USA of preparing for aggression by building up the military strength of South Vietnam, did not take a very belligerent line, presumably because their "peaceful co-existence" diplomacy was achieving further successes elsewhere.

Expressions of China's hostility to the West became stronger after the unrest in Eastern Europe during late 1956. It seemed evident however that the Chinese were not anxious to precipitate a crisis with the West because of the internal and external difficulties facing the USSR, because the USSR's loss of prestige had increased their own opportunities for "peaceful co-existence" diplomacy in South and South-East Asia, and because they were about to purge their own regime.

During most of 1957, and especially about the time when the "anti-party group" was being purged in the USSR, the Chinese avoided increasing their pressures against the West[14]: for example they did not react very strongly after the British, French and US support to the Laotian government in April 1957 against Pathet Lao demands for acceptance of Chinese Communist economic aid. But after launching of the Soviet earth satellites in October and November 1957 the Chinese evidently

13 Speech to National Peoples Congress, NCNA, 30 July 1955.
14 See Political Resolution of 20 March 1957 by National Committee of Chinese Peoples Political Consultative Conference, *People's Daily*, Peking, 21 March 1957.

concluded that the balance of power had shifted decisively in favour of the Communist countries and their attitude towards the West became more aggressive. Following the Iraq coup in July 1958 the Chinese Communist authorities called for vigorous and uncompromising hostility to the "imperialists"; they declared that such hostility would force the West into a continual retreat, and they showed bitterness towards certain "soft-hearted advocates of peace" who were reluctant to undertake vigorous struggles against the West.[15]

In line with their aggressive strategy the Chinese launched a campaign of national mobilisation for the seizure of Taiwan immediately after the resolution of the Middle East crisis in August 1958, and they appeared to be determined to face hostilities with the USA in the Taiwan Straits in order to gain control of the island. In the event, however, no determined effort was made even to gain control of Quemoy, although that island was heavily bombarded, and the danger of direct conflict with US vessels escorting convoys to within a certain distance of Quemoy was avoided. Subsequently the Chinese appeared to have lost some confidence about the military superiority of the Communist countries, for they concluded that the "disintegration" of the "imperialists" might extend "over a fairly long period."[16]

During 1959 however the Chinese apparently decided firmly in favour of vigorous opposition to the West, while opposing the conciliatory Soviet diplomacy which seemed intended to promote a settlement with the "imperialists." Chinese advocacy of intense belligerence towards the West became particularly forthright during 1960, and as has been seen, this was a subject of dispute with the USSR. Nevertheless the Chinese did not take any course of action which would have meant acceptance of increased risks of conflict with the West.

15 See *People's Daily*, Peking, editorials, 4 and 8 August 1958.
16 See Communique of Chinese Communist Party's Central Committee, 10 December 1958 (NCNA, 17 December 1958).

CHAPTER 4

Ideology

Chinese Communist statements on foreign affairs have usually focussed on the regime's current situation and immediate aims, which have been presented in doctrinal terms, but with many points of the ideology stated briefly or left implicit. Since 1953 many of these points have been related not to the final victory of world communism but to a situation of "peaceful co-existence." The use of this term plays on its popular connotation, implying a relaxation of tension and a development of goodwill between the Communist countries and the West. In the esoteric explanations of doctrine however the term refers to a situation in which the Western countries are deterred from "aggression" against the Communist powers while the struggle to promote Communism in individual countries continues. This explanation presupposes acceptance of the doctrinal point that the Western countries are "aggressive" by nature.

Because of their contemporary focus, the major Chinese Communist statements on foreign affairs have reflected some broad changes in the emphasis of the ideological commitment in China's external relations, as well as in the role of the interim objective of "peaceful co-existence." Briefly, there were vigorous expressions of opposition to the West and fairly open support for the insurgent South-East Asian Communist movements until about 1954. China then began to emphasise the promotion of "peaceful co-existence" in Asia, while continuing her opposition to the West, although with slight moderation and while de-emphasising her support of the Asian Communist movements. But in 1958 hostility to the West became stronger and later a demanding attitude was adopted towards the neutral countries which had accepted "peaceful co-existence," while support for Communist revolutionary action in Asia became more open. An example of the first period was Premier Chou En-lai's statement on foreign affairs to the National Committee of the Chinese Peoples Political Consultative Conference on 2 November 1951, which, after long denunciations of the US "imperialists," and especially of their part in the Korean War, reaffirmed China's faith in the insurgent struggles of the other Asian Communist movements:

"Under the influence of the success of the Chinese revolution, the level of consciousness of the Asian people has been raised to an unprecedented degree and liberation movements are developing more and more strongly with each passing day. The unity of the Chinese people and the peoples of Asia will certainly create a powerful and matchless force in the Far East which will rapidly push forward the great wheel of history in the movement for independence and liberation of the peoples of the Asian countries."[1]

The tone of the 1954-8 period was illustrated by Chou En-lai's speeches to the National Peoples Congress on 23 September 1954, 30 July 1955, 28 June 1956, and 26 June 1957.[2] These speeches reflected:

1954   stress on extension of "peaceful co-existence" in Asia, in opposition to Western and especially US attempts to establish SEATO;

1955   attacks on USA for "occupation" of Taiwan, but emphasis on settlement of international disputes by negotiation;

1956   efforts to stir up Afro-Asian opinion against Western "colonial" powers; restrained opposition to West, linked with declarations of willingness to negotiate with KMT for "liberation" of Taiwan; assertions that China has become a great power, able to influence the "entire international situation";

1957   emphasis on strengthening unity with the Communist

1 NCNA, 6 November 1951.
2 NCNA, 23 September 1954, 30 July 1955, 28 June 1956, 26 June 1957.

countries and rallying all uncommitted forces against the "imperialists," so as to force them to accept "peaceful co-existence."

The increased hostility towards the West which developed in 1958 was illustrated in Chou En-lai's review of foreign affairs at the National Peoples Congress during February of that year.[3] Chou En-lai claimed that as a result of Soviet advances in rocketry the international situation had moved decisively in favour of the Communist countries, and that success in the struggle against "imperialism" was thus assured; for the capitalist countries, "peaceful co-existence" with the Communist states was not only possible but "necessary." If the US did not accept peaceful co-existence, its international position would continue to weaken, and if it attempted war it would be destroyed. The "imperialists," especially the USA, would have to agree to overall negotiations with the Communist countries. In August 1958 the Chinese began urging that Communist countries should continue mounting pressures against the West in order to force a continual weakening of the Western position.[4]

The more demanding attitude of the Chinese towards the neutral countries was reflected in Chou En-lai's remarks on foreign policy to the National Peoples Congress on 18 April 1959; he warned against "imperialist" intrigue to sabotage the "solidarity" between the newly-independent countries and the Communist states, and declared that those countries would have to frustrate such plans. Meanwhile he pledged support of the Afro-Asian and Latin American "independence" struggles "to the full extent of our capabilities."

Practice

The actual handling of China's foreign relations has naturally accorded with the general pattern of foreign policy statements, although not entirely. In the first period of open encouragement of revolutionary violence by Asian Communist movements, large scale aid was extended to the Communist-led nationalist insurgents in Indochina, the Viet Minh, and Chinese Communist

3 NCNA, 11 February 1958.
4 *People's Daily*, Peking, editorials, 4 and 8 August 1958.

writings were widely circulated in South and South-East Asia, but assistance to the insurgent Burmese, Malayan and Filippino Communist Parties was evidently restricted to the provision of some propaganda materials, finance, and tactical guidance.[5] The Chinese presumably desired to concentrate their support in one area—Indochina—since the danger of Western retaliation against China herself would have been greater if they had simultaneously given large scale assistance to all the other Communist struggles in South-East Asia. Moreover, only limited aid to the Burmese Communist Party may have seemed feasible because of that body's disunity, and the smuggling of aid to the Malayan and Filippino Communist movements must have been rather difficult.

The campaign for "peaceful co-existence" which began in 1954 reflected increased interest in strengthening China's prestige and security, especially in so far as this enabled a concentration of national energies on the first five-year plan. Meanwhile there was a slackening of overt support to the other Asian communist movements, so as to facilitate cultivation of the goodwill of the established Asian governments, especially with a view to discouraging Asian support for SEATO. But the promotion of cordial relations with other Asian states was also accompanied by expanding Chinese "popular diplomacy" towards the general public in those states, and this indirectly helped expansion by the local Communist movements in several of those countries.

Notwithstanding their increased militancy towards the West in late 1957 and early 1958 the Chinese were evidently not anxious to accept the risk of a major conflict with the "Imperialists." Although they made a show of their determination to seize Taiwan, the Chinese Communist authorities avoided precipitating direct clashes with US forces in the Taiwan Straits. Nevertheless during 1959 the Chinese continued to advocate strong militancy towards the West, and this was intensified in 1960. The encouragement of revolutionary action by Communist movements in the under-developed countries also became pronounced.

---

[5] Capt. M. Kennedy, *A History of Communism in East Asia*, Frederick A. Praeger, New York, 1957, pp. 383 and 452.

Ideology

Attitude to Doctrine

The ideological commitment has thus dominated the handling of China's foreign relations since 1949, but in recent years preoccupation with the regime's national interests has also been apparent, with some doctrinal basis because of the extensive responsibilities for China in the promotion of Communism among the Asian countries. Initially, the present leaders of the Chinese Communist Party evidently accepted this doctrine as a kind of faith, because of its ostensibly comprehensive philosophy, and as a discipline which promised a way of national regeneration for China. The latter was the main theme in many of the writings of Mao Tse-tung during the struggle for supremacy: through Communism China was to become a strong power, put an end to the humiliation and oppression which she had endured from Western imperialism since early in the 19th century, and take part in the elimination of "imperialism" and the establishment of a global Communist system.[6] A Chinese Communist author looking back in 1959 wrote:

> "Imperialism's savage aggression and oppression engendered hatred in the heart of the Chinese people, forcing the advanced elements of China to seek the truth of national salvation, and prompting the Chinese people to unite. The truth of national salvation which the Chinese people found was Marxism-Leninism."[7]

Faith in the guidance of Marxism-Leninism has continued to be evident in Chinese Communist pronouncements, but for some years increasing emphasis has been placed on the "creative" development of Marxism-Leninism by Mao Tse-tung. On the 10th anniversary of the foundation of the Chinese Communist government, the Head of State, Liu Shao-chi, declared:

> "China's lightning speed in developing its social productive forces cannot be matched by any capitalist country and it certainly could never be dreamt of in old China.

[6] See especially the list of Western acts of aggression against China in *The Chinese Revolution and the Chinese Communist Party*, published by Mao Tse-tung in 1939 —Foreign Languages Press, Peking, 1954.

[7] *People's Daily*, Peking, 16 September 1959.

"... In China, without the democratic revolution that overthrew imperialism, feudalism and bureaucrat-capitalism, without the socialist revolution that abolished the capitalist system, there could be no rapid progress of modern industry, modern agriculture and modern science and culture; no situation as the one that prevails today when the people of the whole country are working for the cause of Communism vigorously and resolutely. Revolution has brought the Chinese people boundless hope and an extremely brilliant future.

"The victory of the Chinese people in the past ten years is the victory of the Chinese Communist Party, and the victory of the general lines of the Chinese Communist Party for socialist revolution and for social construction.

"... All our victories are fresh confirmations of, and fresh victories for, Marxism-Leninism. ...

"The Chinese Communist Party, which has led the Chinese Revolution to victory, is armed with Marxism-Leninism; this is epitomized in the famous words of Mao Tse-tung: The integration of the universal truth of Marxism-Leninism with the concrete practice of the Chinese Revolution."[8]

The international significance of China's resurgence through Communism has continued to receive emphasis: China's humiliations in foreign affairs have ended[9] and China has been able to support Communist struggles in the under-developed countries:

"The Chinese people have always considered their revolution as part of the world socialist revolution. ...

"The Chinese people see in all oppressed nations their own yesterday. . . . In the past ten years the Chinese people together with the people of all other countries of the socialist camp headed by the Soviet Union have rendered every support and aid within their capability to every struggle of the people of the Asian, African and Latin American countries to win and defend national independence, democracy and freedom."[10]

8 *People's Daily*, Peking, 1 October 1959.

9 See article by Fang Ch'ao quoted in *Union Research Service*, issue Vol. 17, No. 25, p. 372.

10 Foreign Minister Ch'en Yi, NCNA, 3 October 1959.

Quotations such as these naturally cannot be regarded as completely reliable evidence of the outlook of the Chinese. It goes without saying that, as in other Communist systems, manifestations of ideological conformity in the upper levels of the Chinese Communist Party are undoubtedly bound up with manoeuvrings in highly complicated rivalries over questions of interest and policy. There have certainly been indications of differences over domestic and foreign policy in the upper levels of the Party, as illustrated for example by the long campaign against "right opportunists." Yet there have been no positive signs of a weakening of fidelity to the ideology in the higher levels of the Party. Although it seems reasonable to conclude that these levels must have been affected by the general loss of interest in Communist doctrine about which Mao Tse-tung complained in 1957,[11] their faith in Communism has undoubtedly been sustained by convictions about its domestic potential for social mobilisation and its external significance as a doctrine associated with foreign revolutionary movements through which a restoration of China's ancient political dominance in Asia may be achieved.

International Outlook

The international outlook derived from Marxism-Leninism by the Chinese Communist Party focuses on China's role in the establishment of world Communism. The victory of Communism in China constituted a great extension of the communist system, and in that system China ranks after the USSR and has a special responsibility for encouraging and guiding Communist revolutions in the under-developed countries.

Most expositions of the Chinese Communist Party's international outlook have been along the lines of that given by Teng Hsiao-ping, General Secretary of the Party's Central Committee, on 2 October 1959:

"The Chinese Revolution is a component part of the socialist revolution of the world proletariat. It is a continuation of the great October Revolution. . . . It is an extremely heavy blow

11 Mao Tse-tung, speech on Contradictions, NCNA, 18 June 1957.

to the imperialist system. Victorious new China joined the socialist camp headed by the great Soviet Union and greatly added to the ascendancy of the world socialist system . . . the Chinese people have carried the anti-imperialist and anti-feudal democratic revolution to the end, and through the socialist revolution and construction are rapidly getting rid of poverty and backwardness. . . . This cannot but tremendously inspire all the oppressed nations in their struggle for national liberation, peoples' democracy and a socialist future.

"The great unity of the Soviet Union, China and all the socialist countries and the great unity of the peoples of the whole world are something imperialism and the reactionaries of all countries cannot disrupt. . . . In the face of our great unity, any struggles on the part of imperialism and the re-actionaries will not save them from inevitable destruction. The forces of peace will certainly triumph over the imperialist forces of war; the oppressed nations will certainly overthrow the reactionary rule of colonialism; the socialist system will certainly replace the capitalist system."[12]

In this presentation, however, the acknowledgment of the Soviet Union's leadership of the Communist countries appears to have been a formality, China's responsibilities for promoting the advance of Communism in the under-developed countries have been understated, and the need for vigorous struggles against "imperialism" has not been given the prominence which it began to receive in 1960.

Since 1957 the Chinese have given little recognition to Soviet leadership of the international Communist system; after early 1960 they appeared to have given up all deference to the USSR.[13] China's responsibilities for and interest in the Communist struggles in the under-developed countries have usually received rather evasive treatment in statements of doctrine or policy, but they were presented more openly in 1960. The main Chinese discourse on the November-December 1960 Moscow conference of world Communist Parties reiterated that all

---

12 *People's Daily*, Peking, 2 October 1959.
13 There was no reference to Soviet leadership in Chinese Communist commentaries on the anniversary of the Sino-Soviet Alliance, 14 February 1961.

Communist countries should "energetically support" the "liberation" movements in Africa, Asia and Latin America, and declared that the Chinese Communist regime "constantly pays attention" to those movements.[14]

Chinese Communist pronouncements on foreign affairs have in general accorded with the Soviet view that the international Communist struggle will be victorious either through the defeat of the Western "imperialists" in a global war or through a progressive weakening of the Western position by the expansion of Communism in the under-developed countries and in some of the Western powers.

The USSR, although claiming that the Communist countries would be victorious in a world war, has acknowledged that in such a conflict great damage would be suffered by both sides, and this has been the basis of its preference for achieving world revolution not through global war but through "peaceful co-existence." Explanations of this preference which have been addressed to Western public opinion—for example, Krushchev's article on Peaceful Co-existence in *Foreign Affairs*, October 1959 —have held out the prospect of the Communist countries and the West agreeing to renounce the use of force against each other while the advance of Communism in the under-developed regions and in the West proceeds with Soviet encouragement.

But Soviet explanations of the *doctrine* of "peaceful co-existence," intended for esoteric communication to other Communists, have made it clear that the Western countries, which are regarded as imperialistic by "nature," and which are believed to be plotting "aggression" against the Communist states, are not expected to voluntarily renounce their war potential but must be deterred from aggression by the superior military power of the Communist countries. The exercise of that military superiority will prevent attack on the Communist states by the West and also discourage Western opposition to the expansion of Communism. "Peaceful co-existence" is thus not in conflict with the struggle for world Communism but is a "special form" of that struggle.

The Soviet doctrine on "peaceful co-existence" was expounded

14 *Red Flag* editorial, NCNA, 15 December 1960.

at some length in the Declaration issued by representatives of the world Communist parties in Moscow on 6 December 1960, in terms which accorded with the most recent handbook of Soviet Communism:[15]

"... It is possible to stop the attempts of the imperialist aggressors to unleash a world war. World war can be prevented by the united efforts of the world socialist camp, the international working class, the national liberation movements of all countries that are against war . . . the preponderance of the forces of socialism, peace and democracy becomes ever more evident. . . .

"The unshakable basis of the foreign policy of the socialist countries is the Leninist principle of 'peaceful co-existence' and economic competition between socialist and capitalist countries. Under conditions of peace the socialist system is developing more and more extensively its superiority over the capitalist system in all fields. . . . The near future will bring new successes to the forces of peace and socialism. The USSR will be transformed into the greatest industrial power in the world. China will become a mighty industrial country. . . . The zones of peace will become even more extensive. The workers' movement in the colonies and dependent countries* will gain new victories. The decay in the colonial system will be completed. The superiority of the forces of socialism and peace will become absolute. Under these conditions, even before the complete victory of socialism on the earth, and while capitalism is still preserved in parts of the world a real opportunity will arise to rule out world war from the life of society.

". . . Peaceful co-existence among States does not mean, as the revisionists assert, a rejection of the class war. Co-existence between States of differing social systems is a form of class struggle between socialism and capitalism. *In conditions of peaceful co-existence, favourable opportunities are created for developing the class struggle in capitalist countries and the*

---

15 Tass, 6 December 1960, and *Fundamentals of Marxism-Leninism*, Foreign Languages Publishing House, Moscow (undated, but apparently 1959).

* Standard reference to the under-developed countries.

*national liberation movement of peoples in colonial and dependent countries.** In turn the successes of the revolutionary class and the national liberation struggle contribute to the consolidation of peaceful co-existence. Communists consider it their duty to strengthen the faith of the popular masses in the possibility of strengthening peaceful co-existence, and their determination to avert world war. They will help the peoples in every way, in their active struggle for peace, democracy and national liberation, *increasingly weakening and narrowing the positions of imperialism."**

Although the Chinese endorsed this Declaration, their own pronouncements on the question of "peaceful co-existence" with the West had been at variance with it. They had called for unrelenting pressures against the West and for the expansion of Communism, and had argued against moderating such pressures in order to avoid war. Thus an editorial in the *People's Daily*, Peking, of 8 August 1958 had stressed the aggressive nature of the "imperialists" and had declared that it was necessary to struggle resolutely and uncompromisingly against them, otherwise they would become daring. Even if the West did begin a war the result would be a Communist victory. All opposition to the West constituted a struggle for "peace"; it was naive to believe that the West should not be "provoked" for the sake of peace, and "groundless" to conclude "that peace can be gained only when there is no armed resistance against the attacks of the imperialists and the colonists and when there is no bitter struggle against them." Peace had to be "fought for" and not "begged" from the "imperialists": any compromise in dealing with those "imperialists" would end in "submission."

This doctrine of unrelenting pressures against the West had been further expounded by the Chinese during 1960. There was no prospect of a satisfactory settlement with the West, unrelenting pressures against the "imperialists" would have to be maintained, and war against these "imperialists" was highly probable but was not to be feared. The "imperialists" had not changed their "nature"—it was "inconceivable" that they would accept a

* Emphasis added.

proposal for general and complete disarmament[16]—and to moderate the international Communist struggle against the West through fear of a global war would be folly:

> ". . . The proletariat in the socialist countries must, with the assistance of the world proletariat and the working masses of the oppressed nations, defend the fruits of victory which the proletarian revolution has already achieved, and, at the same time, *support the continuous advance of the cause of proletarian revolution in other countries,** continuously diminishing the strength of imperialism until capitalism has perished and socialism has triumphed throughout the world.
>
> ". . . The modern revisionists are panic-stricken by the imperialist policy of nuclear war blackmail. They develop from fear of war to fear of revolution, and proceed from not wanting revolution themselves to opposing other people's carrying out revolution."[17]

In order to dissipate fears of nuclear war, the Chinese asserted that the decisive factor in all armed conflicts was the will of the "people." They conceded, however, that the military power of the West was a reality and they implied that pressures against "imperialism" *would* have to be graduated. This doctrine was set out in connection with the issue of the 4th volume of Mao Tse-tung's works during late 1960.

Mao Tse-tung's military doctrine, as expounded by commentators, emphasised that to undertake war against "imperialism" was entirely "just" and necessary: in order to attain permanent peace, war had to be waged against "imperialism" to finally destroy it and thus bridge the way to "a new world." War was not to be feared, despite the military power of the "imperialists," because the decisive factor in armed conflict was ideological commitment, which was present only on the Communist side. But nevertheless full account had to be taken of the real military potential of the "imperialists," and thus the Communist forces

16 Liu Chang-sheng to WFTU Executive Bureau, NCNA, 8 June 1960.
17 Lu Ting-i at Peking Rally, NCNA, 22 April 1960
* Emphasis added.

46

were to be preserved, there was to be no reckless acceptance of battle, and victory was to be sought only through many limited engagements, each of which was to be undertaken only if heavy local superiority was assured.[18]

The emphasis of this doctrine on cautious, protracted, limited struggles as the correct way to ultimate victory over the West suggested that the Chinese campaign for unrelenting hostility towards the "imperialists" was not so much a declaration of *China's* willingness to face the risks of a major war as a demand for more militant struggles by the Communist movements *in the under-developed countries* and for a more resolute *Soviet* attitude towards the West. This would explain the bitter Chinese complaint against "revisionists" in the international Communist movement, who through fear of global war were imposing restraints on revolutionary action by other Communist parties.

Chauvinism

The projection of the Chinese line on "peaceful co-existence" was accompanied by the appearance of a chauvinist spirit in China's handling of the Communist ideology. This tended to confirm that the Chinese demands for uncompromising hostility towards the West were part of an overall assertion of China's interests as against the USSR.

The doctrinal perspective which the Chinese originally shared with the Soviet Union had involved a right of primacy for the USSR in the interpretation of Marxism-Leninism and in the direction of the international Communist movement. This double primacy was considered necessary to ensure tight unity and effective co-ordination in the world revolution. But Soviet doctrinal and political primacy could sanction attempts to direct the foreign and domestic affairs of other Communist states in ways which accorded very closely with the national interests of the USSR. The Chinese, in their pronouncement on the unrest in Eastern Europe at the end of 1956, had indicated that such interference had been attempted by the USSR while Stalin was alive:

18 *People's Daily*, Peking, 6 and 7 October 1960; *Nan Fang Jih Pao*, Canton, 3 November 1960; *Red Flag*, 1 October 1960.

"On the whole, in relations with brother countries and parties, Stalin took an internationalist stand and helped the struggle of other peoples and the growth of the socialist camp; but in tackling certain concrete questions, he showed a tendency towards great-nation chauvinism and himself lacked a spirit of equality, let alone educating the mass of cadres to be modest. Sometimes he even intervened mistakenly, with many grave consequences, in the internal affairs of certain brother countries and parties."[19]

The pronouncement implied that China and all other Communist countries would have to be vigilant in order to defeat any future Soviet attempts at interference in their affairs. Meanwhile, the Chinese had apparently concluded that in addition to resisting any Soviet encroachments on their rights they would have to consolidate their independence by displacing Soviet authority in the international Communist movement.

China's rejection of the USSR's double primacy since 1956 has been, increasingly, an expression of chauvinism, and her deepening rivalry with the USSR has made this chauvinism more active. This, inevitably, has led to ideological changes, and in particular to the development of a national focus for ideological loyalties, but with observance of substantial doctrinal continuity.

The chauvinist spirit in China's handling of Marxism-Leninism, which has evidently developed with the need to assert China's interests against the USSR, emphasises China's development into a powerful state and her role in the promotion of world Communism. China's relationship with the USSR is at times presented as one of equal partnership but at other times it is suggested that China is rightfully the leading state in the Communist system. Mao Tse-tung is claimed to be the "greatest Marxist-Leninist of contemporary times"[20] and his strategy for the international revolutionary struggle is the correct one, unlike that of the "revisionists."[21] Meanwhile, Mao Tse-tung's "thought" in effect supplants orthodox Marxism-Leninism:

19 Article on Historical Experience of Proletarian Dictatorship, *People's Daily*, Peking, 29 December 1956.
20 General Fu Chung, *People's Daily*, Peking, 6-7 October 1960.
21 By late 1961 it was evident that the Chinese were using this term for oblique references to the Soviet authorities.

Ideology

"To fulfil the great task of Socialist revolution and construction, the fundamental question is to study and apply Mao Tse-tung's ideology . . . and his method of thinking and working. Comrade Mao Tse-tung has summed up the rich experience in China's revolution and construction and in the international Communist movement. He has, under new historical conditions, inherited, safeguarded and developed Marxism-Leninism. His ideology constitutes the theoretical foundations of the three magic wands of our party—the general line for socialist construction, the big leap forward and the peoples' communes."[22]

Chauvinism has long been recognised as a dominant factor in the psychological make-up of the Han Chinese, and it has evidently exerted stronger influence on the thinking of the Chinese leaders with the consolidation of their regime's international position, which they probably regard as promising restoration of China's former political primacy in Asia. In order to avoid undue provocation to the USSR, however, and to guard against alienating neutral Asian goodwill, the Chinese Communist authorities have almost certainly endeavoured to restrain displays of extreme nationalism in their handling of the Communist ideology. Hence the actual force of chauvinism within that ideology in China is probably stronger than its doctrinal reflections suggest.

During 1956 the Chinese Communist authorities certainly felt that manifestations of chauvinism were harming their relations with other Asian countries. At the 8th Party Congress in September of that year Liu Shao-chi declared that efforts would have to be made to overcome chauvinism in China's dealings with other nations, and Premier Chou En-lai, during his South-East Asian tour in early 1957, claimed that China disapproved of "great nation chauvinism" and was endeavouring to overcome chauvinist tendencies in her relations with other Asian states. Much chauvinism however was apparent in the hostility which the Chinese regime showed towards India in 1959, and there were manifestations of chauvinism in China's denunciations of the Indonesian discrimination against local Chinese traders in 1960.

22 NCNA, 4 June 1960.

The chauvinist influence on ideology in China *could* make for an openness to foreign (non-Communist) thought with a view to selective absorption: in scientific fields some such openness has already been apparent, having been called for in 1956[23]. Attention to non-Communist thinking in such fields may well increase, since for nation-building reasons chauvinism may weaken doctrinal controls which are impeding the utilisation of foreign scientific advances. But in the wider fields of economics, philosophy, literature, history and politics the chauvinist influence is unlikely to make for greater receptivity to foreign ideas; on the contrary, it is likely to exclude these all the more vigorously, because it will make for stronger opposition against the emergence of views and attitudes which would hamper social mobilisation. The strong urge towards unity and discipline within the Chinese Communist Party partly expresses a belief that "bourgeois" Western thought works against the emergence of a popular will by tending to produce divisions and conflicts among the people. This theme is implicit in most Chinese Communist denunciations of "revisionist" tendencies in modern Chinese literature which would sanction imitation of "bourgeois" Western writings.[24] In their justification for totalitarian party control in all Communist regimes the Chinese Communist authorities have endorsed Lenin's contempt for bourgeois "diffuseness, instability, incapacity for sustained effort, unity and organised action."[25]

Chauvinism *may* cause some return to traditional Chinese values. There may be some trend towards the achievement of social harmony through a toleration of diversity and reduced emphasis on "struggle." The beginnings of an attempt in this direction were apparent in the somewhat liberal policy towards the intellectuals in 1956, which, although it led into a deceitful encouragement of critics in the 1957 rectification campaign, appears to have begun as a genuine effort to gain more positive support for the regime from the non-Communist intelligentsia, in return for an indulgent attitude towards their "bourgeois"

23 See Chou En-lai's report on the Intellectuals, NCNA, 29 January 1956.
24 See speeches by Chou Yang and Lu Ting-yi at Congress of Writers and Artists, *People's Daily*, Peking, 4 September 1960 and NCNA, 22 July 1960.
25 Pronouncement on Historical Experience of Proletarian Dictatorship, *People's Daily*, Peking, 29 December 1956.

thinking.[26] In recent years the pressure on the intellectuals for ideological conformity has been severe, but the Communist authorities appear to appreciate that such pressures are to a considerable extent counter-productive. Although there have been no indications of a relaxation, some move in that direction may result if the problem is viewed from a less doctrinaire aspect and more in the light of the overall needs of nation-building. The Chinese Communist authorities have shown intense opposition to any search for values outside the crude and limited framework of Marxism-Leninism, and have campaigned relentlessly against all manifestations of "bourgeois" thinking, because "the harmful effects of poisonous bourgeois ideas will be smaller if they are met with resistance and given blows,"[27] but the influence of chauvinism could take the edge off this hostility to non-Communist values. In the interests of nation-building, the Chinese authorities may become convinced of the need to secure more spontaneous popular co-operation by tolerating or promoting a restoration of certain traditional ideals. But, to the extent that pressures for ideological conformity are relaxed, popular resistance to the Party's remaining doctrinal controls will probably increase.

The foreign policy consequences of the chauvinist trend in China's handling of the Communist ideology must be assessed after examination of the role of national interests in her external affairs, and after a study of her relations with the USSR. At this stage, however, it can be anticipated that the securing of external support for China's development and the adoption of strategies for the expansion of China's power will proceed with less regard for orthodox Communist doctrine; that China's services to the international Communist struggle will be more self-interested; and that her handling of foreign affairs will be more self-reliant but possibly more arbitrary and less well-informed. As the loyalty of the Chinese leaders to fundamental Communist doctrine may not be seriously weakened, however, the commitment to support Communist struggles abroad will no doubt remain very strong. Nevertheless it will be impossible to reverse

26 See Chou En-lai's Report on the Intellectuals, NCNA, 29 January 1956.
27 Lu Ting-yi, at the National Congress of Writers and Artists, NCNA, 22 July 1960.

the chauvinist interpretation of Communist teachings in China. China cannot move back towards acceptance of Soviet doctrinal and political primacy, and her leaders undoubtedly believe that if they do not continue to assert their national interests as against the USSR their position will weaken.

CHAPTER 5

National Interests

The handling of China's foreign affairs over the past decade has reflected considerable preoccupation with the advancement of the regime's national interests, within and in some respects to the prejudice of the commitment to promote world Communism. Risks to China's external security have been avoided and attempts have been made to improve that security by building up China's war potential, by maintaining an alliance with the USSR, by discouraging other Asian countries from co-operating with the West, and by giving support to Asian Communist movements — which have promised an extension of China's influence and a contraction of the Western position in Asia. Meanwhile China's economic development has been promoted through reliance on Soviet bloc economic co-operation but also on a basis of significant trade with the West and with other Asian countries, and China has sought to expand her authority and influence, not only for the preservation of her security, but to acquire a powerful and independent role in the building up of the world Communist system.

The concern to avoid risks to China's security has been dictated by the regime's military doctrine and has been evident in the cautious actions which have followed declarations of intent to seize Taiwan, in the limited assistance extended to the Burmese, Malayan, Laotian and other South-East Asian Communist movements, and in China's apparent insistence that North Vietnamese control of the southern part of that country be secured only through indirect aggression.

While avoiding acceptance of serious risks to her security, China has improved her military position by developing her armaments industry, by building up military co-operation with the USSR and by encouraging neutrality in Asia, especially through securing the acceptance of "peaceful co-existence" in India, Burma, Cambodia, Indonesia and Ceylon. It is true that more recent behaviour towards India has provoked *de facto* modifications of that country's neutrality, but it has also increased fear of and respect for China in South-East Asia, and especially in Burma and Cambodia.

China's dependence on the Soviet bloc for assistance in her economic development has been heavy; roughly 75% of her trade has been conducted with that bloc, and she has received considerable economic aid from the USSR, although this support has been small in comparison with her needs and has apparently come slowly. Since 1956 China has increased her imports from the West and these now constitute more than 20% of her purchases from abroad; her trade with other Asian countries has remained small but has reflected a significant dependence on some of their primary exports.

During recent years, a desire to expand China's power and influence, over and above the requirements of her immediate security needs, has evidently contributed to her militant encouragement of other Asian Communist movements, her assertion of independence from and equality with the USSR in the international Communist system, and her endeavours to intervene in Middle Eastern and African affairs. Meanwhile, although external security issues have been very much involved in China's relations with India and Japan, those relations have also reflected attempts to spread China's power.

In considering all the evidence about the influence of national interests in China's foreign policy, some ambiguity arises because of the distinction which must be drawn between *objective* national interests and those national interests which are posited by Communist doctrine; the latter include many of the former, but viewed in a special way. China's national interests are understood in an ideological fashion, but before proceeding to examine that perspective it will be advisable to consider the *objective* national interests to which any modern Chinese government could be expected to be responsive.

Owing to her economic backwardness China does not have a

defence potential commensurate with her size and population and could sustain a major conflict with a modern power only if large-scale external assistance were provided. Hence great emphasis must be placed on the preservation of China's external security and her avoidance of a major war. Any modern Chinese government would thus have to conduct its foreign relations with caution and it would have to secure allies, while using all means short of war to discourage, weaken and isolate any country threatening aggression. Meanwhile such a government would have to overcome as rapidly as possible China's economic backwardness, which prevents her from asserting her interests with adequate power and makes her vulnerable to external pressures as well as unduly dependent on actual or potential supporters. Overcoming this economic backwardness must be largely a matter of securing capital goods from the industrial countries by exports of China's surplus agricultural products, and China would therefore require scope to secure the best possible terms for her sales of agricultural commodities and to exploit competition among the industrial countries in the capital goods market. Meanwhile, China would have to obtain from abroad fuels and raw materials for her new industries and she would need outlets for products coming from those industries, since these would supplement her foreign exchange earnings and reduce the burden on her agriculture.

Finally, a modern Chinese government would have to pay special attention to neighbouring parts of Asia; potential aggressors among the nearby countries would have to be dealt with, and China would have to build up goodwill among other adjacent countries, so as to preclude their co-operation with any hostile power, to discourage the emergence of any local hostility towards herself, and to guarantee her access to their markets. Since China has in the past endured protracted aggression from Japan, any modern Chinese government must have an interest in curbing the restoration of that country's war potential; on the other hand, since China has also experienced encroachments and attempts at political domination by the USSR, assertion of China's independence as against the Soviet Union is also required; but if allies are to be sought in order to strengthen

China against the USSR the advanced western nations would not altogether qualify, for the major West European powers oppressed and humiliated China for long periods in recent history, and the USA, after in effect condoning Japanese aggression against China in the 1930s, required Chinese concessions to the Soviet Union in 1945 in return for Soviet participation in the war against Japan. Meanwhile, since China's security and economic development could be affected by changes in the unstable and vulnerable area of South-East Asia, a modern Chinese government would be expected to establish some influence in this region and to discourage the South-East Asian governments from co-operating too closely with the Western powers, Japan, or the USSR.

Doctrine and National Interests

In contrast with all these objective interests, Communist doctrine presents China's welfare as being set for fulfilment in her own progress towards Communism and in her contribution to world revolution. When global Communism is established, there will be unending international peace, because the source of war—"imperialism"—will have been destroyed. China will thenceforth be liberated from the danger of aggression and her relations with the other Communist States will be—as now—on a basis of equality, mutual respect and mutual benefit, although the possibility of serious deviations from this code of proletarian goodwill will apparently remain.[1] Little other information is available about the state of international relations envisaged in the future world Communist system but this much forms the basis for a doctrine of common interests between all Communist States and movements: as they are all involved in a common struggle, the welfare of each depends on the active support of all the others, and among other things this means that each has an interest in ensuring the fidelity of the others to the doctrines of Marxism-Leninism.[2]

In this ideological perspective, the need to maintain and build

1 Article on Dictatorship of the Proletariat, *People's Daily*, Peking, 29 December 1956.
2 Declaration issued in Moscow by representatives of World Communist Parties, Tass, 6 December 1960.

up China's security is compulsive, as it would be for a non-Communist country, but Communist doctrine imposes an obligation on China to maintain hostility towards the West, and thus to accept certain risks to China's security. Meanwhile, China's nation-building is ordained not only towards her own attainment of the ideal state of "Communism" but also towards her fulfilment of a decisive role in the promotion of international revolutionary movements—which must imply a wider and more thorough-going expansion of her authority than would be envisaged from the aspect of her "objective" national interests.

Because of their commitment to Marxism-Leninism, the Chinese Communist authorities are pledged to oppose "capitalism" and struggle for the advance of Communism. They must oppose the capitalist system with intent to destroy it, without any "illusions" that it may voluntarily undergo any changes in the direction of "socialism," and they must maintain an attitude of hostility towards the leading "capitalist" or "imperialist" countries, so as to

—be prepared for war, which the "imperialists" are planning and may launch at any moment,

—discourage the "imperialists" from "aggression" against the Communist states and against Communist movements struggling for power in areas outside the Sino-Soviet bloc,

—sustain the militancy of Communist movements which are endeavouring to gain power abroad.

All this involves acceptance of significant risks to China's security. But, while this belligerence forces some Western toleration of Chinese or Soviet support to insurgent Communist or Communist led movements in the under-developed countries, a major conflict with the West is to be avoided, and therefore China must retain scope to ease her pressures against the "imperialists." This requirement can be fulfilled by ensuring that demonstrations of hostility to the West are accompanied by assertions of China's desire for "peaceful co-existence." This can sanction a retreat from any belligerent position in order to prevent the risks to China's security from becoming too great, and to prepare the way for such a retreat a limited cultivation of the lesser "imperialist" countries is an obvious strategy to employ.

This is the perspective which Marxism-Leninism gives to China's security. Although continuing to play much of the compulsive role which it would have as an objective national interest for any modern Chinese regime, national security is something to be risked in a strategy of "brinkmanship" in order to promote the international Communist struggle, but in a selective manner so as to divide the "imperialists" and with a retreat to normal "peaceful co-existence" kept open at all times. Meanwhile, Communist doctrine, and in particular the principle of "proletarian internationalism," obliges China to ally herself with the other Communist states and movements and of course precludes any pursuit of security through alliances with any of the "capitalist" states, although continual improvement in China's security can and indeed ought to be pursued through cultivating goodwill among the under-developed countries of Africa and Asia.

Meanwhile Marxism-Leninism gives a special orientation to China's nation-building and lays down certain principles about how it should proceed. China's economy must be developed not only in order to bring her eventually to the stage of "Communism" but also to enable her to contribute more effectively to the struggle against 'imperialism" and the establishment of a world Communist system. In what could be regarded as the orthodox ideological perspective, the pattern for China's nation-building is the Soviet Union, and external measures to promote China's economic development should be consistent with her obligation to the international Communist movement. The latter point is implicit in the general body of Marxism-Leninism; it has not been interpreted as excluding trade with the West but it has been considered to oblige each Communist country to conduct most of its trade with the other Communist states and it has been regarded as ruling out acceptance of any Western economic aid, although the denunciations aimed at Yugoslavia on this account have not been directed against Poland. Communist doctrine insists on a subordination of a Communist state's external economic policy to the international Communist struggle, and in general excludes pursuit of economic advantages by any Communist country through compromise with the "imperialists."

Finally, Marxism-Leninism in effect provides a new way of extending China's power in South-East Asia. The Chinese have advanced their revolution as a model for the under-developed countries and they have also made it clear that they feel a responsibility for ensuring fidelity to Marxism-Leninism in the international Communist movement as a whole.

All this illustrates what might be called the orthodox ideological understanding of China's national interests, but to appreciate the real influence exerted by those interests on China's foreign policy it is necessary to examine the ways in which the chauvinist spirit in Chinese Communist doctrine alters the perception of those interests. It undoubtedly makes for more caution in matters affecting China's external security, for a more exclusive concern with China's economic development, and for greater emphasis on the expansion of China's power.

Chauvinism and National Interests

Under the heading of external security, the chauvinist influence in doctrine must reduce China's willingness to accept military dependence on the USSR or to face significant risks of major conflict with a modern power. In the orthodox ideological perspective, China's alliance with the USSR should enable her to face greater risks in maintaining pressures against the West, especially through assistance to foreign Communist movements, but Chinese chauvinism must be opposed to any unavoidable reliance on the USSR for military support, because of a fear that the USSR would exploit such dependence, and meanwhile this chauvinism must cause obligations to the international Communist struggle to appear considerably less important than China's continued security. China's *attitude* towards the West may become more hostile, due to the influence of chauvinism, but this will not alter the need for greater caution about the acceptance of real hazards to China's strategic position.

The increased caution about accepting real risks to China's

security must make for greater emphasis on the expansion of China's influence through securing the co-operation of existing governments elsewhere in Asia as well as through support to Communist or Communist-led dissident movements in other Asian countries. At the same time this caution must also result in increased real although not necessarily overt readiness to compromise on specific issues with the West. But while calling for greater caution about facing risks to China's security chauvinism must lead to resolute determination to expand China's power and it must thus demand stronger demonstrations of China's authority and of her hostility towards those states which impede her ascendancy in Asia.

Meanwhile, the orthodox ideological understanding of China's need for national development must be considerably changed by the influence of chauvinism. There must be little disposition to regard China's nation-building as subordinate to the international Communist struggle and accordingly there is probably a tendency to trade more with the West, so as to utilise whatever advantages the West may offer in comparison with the USSR as a source of capital goods. On the other hand, chauvinism also probably results in stronger Chinese demands for increased assistance from the USSR, although at the same time the Chinese must presumably become reluctant to accept substantial economic dependence on the Soviet Union.

Chauvinism, in conflict with the internationalist spirit in the orthodox doctrine of Marxism-Leninism, presumably makes for opposition to any integration of China's economy with that of the Soviet Union or other Communist states. Chinese Communist economic policy statements, especially in recent years, have usually reflected intentions of building up an independent economic system in China, and although China has frequently been represented at meetings of the Warsaw Pact's Council For Mutual Economic Assistance she has declined economic coordination with the other Communist states. China has presumably seen, in the Council for Mutual Economic Assistance, an attempt by the USSR to set up a Soviet-controlled economic system embracing all the Communist countries, and in any case she has probably not been impressed by the quality of the economic co-ordination so far achieved under the auspices of that Council.[3]

In order to secure capital goods, China has relied heavily on trade with the USSR and Eastern Europe and she has obtained considerable Soviet economic aid. But China has also traded with Western Europe and in recent years her imports from that area have greatly increased. Few reliable details about China's foreign trade are available, owing to the reticence of the Chinese Communist government on this subject, but according to UN estimates her exports in 1955-7 averaged US $1453.7 million and her imports US $1246.7 million, Soviet Bloc shares being about 64% and 75%.[4] According to Soviet figures China's imports from the Soviet Union in 1959 were R3818 million compared with R2536 million in 1958, while her exports to the USSR rose to R4401 million in 1959 compared with R3525 million in 1958.[5] Meanwhile, China's imports from Western Europe rose from US $72.8 million in 1955 to US $420.5 million in 1958, i.e., a level about one-third below her imports from the Soviet Union in that year.

The trend towards increasing imports from Western Europe continued in 1960. In the same year, China's imports from the USSR may have also increased considerably, but if China has become relatively more dependent on imports from Western Europe this may reflect dissatisfaction with the USSR as a trading partner. The USSR has probably endeavoured to profit from its trade with China, since China has been the weaker partner and the type of trade necessitated by China's backwardness is basically unattractive to the Soviet Union, for the USSR can itself use many of the capital goods which it provides to China and does not require large quantities of Chinese agricultural produce.[6]

China has been receiving economic aid from the Soviet Union since 1950, but the construction of Soviet industrial projects in China has lagged[7] and the volume of assistance has been small

3 See Economic Integration, Problems and Prospects, by Alfred Zauberman, *Problems of Communism*, July-August 1959, and CMEA: A Progress Report, also by Zauberman, *Problems of Communism*, July-August 1960.
4 *Direction of International Trade*, UN Statistical papers, Series T, Vol. X, No. 8.
5 Vneshnyaya Torgovlya SSR 1959.
6 *Moscow-Peking Axis*, Council on Foreign Relations, New York 1957, p. 83.
7 1959 Economic Plan report, NCNA, 21 April 1959.

in relation to China's needs, has reflected little preference for her in comparison with Soviet aid to the non-Communist under-developed countries, and has been less in value than the flow of Western aid to India.

The influence of chauvinism on the appreciation of China's obligation to promote Communism abroad must make for greater emphasis on the expansion of China's power within that commitment and hence for special attention to nearby parts of Asia, and especially the vulnerable region of South-East Asia. The establishment of Communist governments loyal to China in the countries to her south would represent a recovery of China's former imperial authority in this region, guarantee her access to its rich resources and presumably space for her colonizing enterprise, while pre-empting the region from the USSR and improving China's security as against the West. Meanwhile, chauvinism must incline the Chinese to further build up their influence in the international Communist system.

If Marxism-Leninism were interpreted only according to the apparent wishes of the USSR it would require the Chinese to work for the establishment of Soviet-orientated Communist states in other parts of Asia, with China's legitimate interest in the matter being restricted to the security aspect *vis-à-vis* the West. This however is clearly not the way in which the Chinese see the issue. A desire to recover the influence which imperial China once had over much of South-East Asia was reflected in Mao Tse-tung's writings during the 1930s[8] and was implied in the projection of Chinese Communism as a model for the other Asian countries in 1949, as well as in more recent, although less specific, expositions of this theme.[9]

In the present context of Asian international relations any Chinese Communist claim to suzerainty over a large part of South-East Asia, on a basis of former imperial rights, would be out of the question, since China has given much expression to

8 Mao Tse-tung, *The Chinese Revolution and the Chinese Communist Party*, 1939; original text as quoted by Robert C. North in *Moscow and the Chinese Communists*, Stanford University Press, 1953, p. 272.

9 *Communism in South-East Asia*, J. H. Brimmell, Oxford University Press, 1959, p. 259; see also references indicating encouragement to Communist revolutionary struggles in the under-developed countries which appeared in Chinese Communist commentaries on Mao Tse-tung's works during October-November 1960.

her recognition of the independence of several of the South-East Asian countries. The projection of China's revolution as a model for Asia, however, is appropriate for the circumstances since the Chinese claim to leadership over the other Asian Communist movements is only implicit.

After 1949 the Chinese appeared to have built up considerable influence among the Communist movements in South-East Asia, but since 1955 the USSR has evidently been endeavouring to direct the loyalties of those movements entirely towards itself. A test of the orientation of the South-East Asian Communist Parties was provided at the November-December 1960 meeting of representatives of the international Communist movement in Moscow, at which only the Indonesian Communist Party is reported to have endorsed the belligerent strategy towards the West which the Chinese had been advocating in opposition to the USSR.

Soviet opposition to the expansion of their authority in Asia by indirect aggression must be a major factor for the Chinese to consider, since China's national interests are vulnerable to Soviet pressures in other important respects: China is still very much dependent on trade with the USSR and Eastern Europe, and will have to rely very much on Soviet military support in the event of war. The pursuit of China's national interests in any respect which may court Soviet opposition must be subject to calculations about the extent to which the USSR is able to pressure China on other matters.

Meanwhile, although the Chinese have in recent years taken a more demanding attitude towards the neutral Asian countries, they must still be influenced by short-term strategic considerations about the value of those countries' neutral foreign policies. China's security requires that such countries should not be provoked into close co-operation with the West, but there would clearly be a danger of this occurring if the Chinese gave strong open support to insurgent activities by their local Communist movements—unless those movements were assured of quick success. Since several of the neutral Asian countries are extremely afraid of China's power, however, the Chinese have scope to support insurgent Communist movements in those countries by limited measures short of provoking the threatened governments to seek protection from the West. Provided that there does not seem to be any immediate danger of success by such a movement, limited Chinese support to it may well appear a lesser danger to the government of the target country than the outright hostility and heavy military pressure which it would have to face from China if it sought Western assistance.

While giving stronger motivation to China's expansion in Asia, the chauvinist influence operating within their ideology must impel the Chinese to strengthen and consolidate their position in the international Communist system as a whole, especially so as to compete with the USSR for the leadership of the Communist states and movements. The Chinese have asserted parity with the USSR in the leadership of the international Communist system, but they have not managed to expand the influence which they gained in East Europe during 1956-7 and they have apparently not succeeded in their attempts to displace Soviet authority in North Korea or Mongolia, while in North Vietnam their influence is apparently giving way before that of the USSR. Meanwhile, in the international Communist movement generally the Chinese have gained little support for their opposition to the Soviet line on "peaceful co-existence" with the West.

In general the chauvinist trend in China's ideology undoubtedly reduces Chinese respect for the independence of other Communist states and must make for a willingness to utilise other Communist movements as means towards the fulfilment of China's interests. Similar tendencies have long been apparent in Soviet foreign policy, but the USSR has possessed the doctrinal authority needed to sanction such behaviour, and the influence of chauvinism in Soviet foreign relations has been less intense than the preoccupation with national ambitions which now appears to be developing in China.

CHAPTER 6

Alignment with the USSR

Alliance with the USSR has been a fundamental principle of China's foreign policy and until recently her diplomacy and external news comments were entirely co-ordinated with those of the USSR. From alliance with the USSR China has acquired much security, considerable economic and military assistance, and scope to improve her international position. On the other hand, the protection has undoubtedly been conditional and has not been such as to reduce very greatly the cautions imposed on China's foreign policy by her economic backwardness; meanwhile, the volume of economic assistance has not been adequate for China's needs and has reflected only a limited preference for China as against the non-Communist under-developed countries.

The alliance with the USSR was initially based on ideological agreement with the Soviet regime. But the Soviet Union's ambition to build up monolithic unity in the international Communist system, under its own leadership, with some neglect of the interests of other Communist states and movements, was almost certainly a provocation to the Chinese, and since 1956 it has been clear that Soviet primacy in the international Communist movement is no longer really acceptable to China.

When a Chinese Communist delegation led by Mao Tse-tung went to Moscow in December 1949 to negotiate on questions of co-operation between the two countries the Chinese were evidently obliged to determine their attitude towards a number of practical issues in which their interests were clearly at stake. The Soviet Union was in effect controlling Mongolia as a satellite, had obtained concessions in Manchuria in accordance with the Yalta Agreement, and had resumed its long-standing efforts to penetrate Sinkiang; in addition, the Soviet Union had removed or destroyed many industrial installations in Manchuria, for which China was presumably entitled to ask for compensation.

Under a Treaty of Friendship, Alliance and Mutual Assistance, announced on 14 February 1950, each side pledged to co-operate with the other in all actions aimed at promoting international peace and security, and to develop economic and cultural ties between the two countries. Both partners were to take all necessary measures to prevent aggression against either by Japan, or any other state in collaboration with Japan, and each was to give immediate assistance to the other in the event of an attack on either by Japan or any state united with her.[1] The "other power" was clearly the United States of America, which then had considerable armed forces occupying Japan. For China the Treaty reduced the risks which otherwise would have had to be faced if she were to attempt military expansion into Taiwan or elsewhere in Asia, while for the USSR the Treaty improved the security of the Soviet Far East.

An agreement related to the Treaty permitted the Soviet Union to continue using Port Arthur Naval Base and the Chinese Changchung Railway, pending the conclusion of a peace treaty with Japan but not beyond the end of 1952. The question of Dairen was to be reconsidered on the conclusion of a peace treaty with Japan, but meanwhile the administration of the port was to be in the hands of the Chinese. The Soviet Union had secured the right to use Port Arthur and the Chinese Changchung Railway from the Chinese Nationalist Government in 1945.

The Treaty's provision for economic co-operation was put into effect by an agreement which promised China a Soviet credit of US $300 million over five years, subject to repayment within ten years from the end of 1954 with interest at 1%. This agreement was announced on the same date as the Treaty and then in March a number of Sino-Soviet joint stock companies were formed, two for the exploitation of mineral resources in Sinkiang, one to operate an airline between China and the Soviet Union, and another to engage in ship building. In April a Sino-

---

1 *Documents on International Affairs 1949-50*, Royal Institute of International Affairs, London, p. 541.

Soviet Trade Agreement was announced, together with an agreement on exchanges of commodities during 1950.

Exchanges of notes in connection with the Treaty promised China restoration of the property which the USSR had confiscated from the Japanese after its advance into Manchuria in 1945, but China recognised the "independence" of the Mongolian People's Republic. The Chinese leaders were presumably reluctant to agree to this latter step because at the 2nd National Congress of the Chinese Communist Party in July 1922 it had been agreed to work for the "liberation" of Mongolia and its incorporation into a "Federal Chinese Republic."[2] Chinese Communist maps issued since 1950 have shown much of the Sino-Mongolian border as unsettled, although the USSR evidently regards the boundary as fixed.[3]

The Treaty's provisions for the co-ordination of Sino-Soviet external policies in the interests of peace and security had already been evident in the Chinese Communist Government's handling of foreign relations. In this respect the Treaty simply gave expression to the principle of alignment with the Soviet Union which had been laid down in Mao Tse-tung's writings before the establishment of the Communist Government in Peking.

The cultural co-operation provided for under the Treaty was soon evident in the popularising of Soviet achievements in Chinese Communist newspapers and radio programmes as well as in the Chinese education system. In all this China may have been under some Soviet pressure, for among the Chinese generally there had been an antipathy towards the Russians, and adulation of the USSR cut across the appeal to nationalist sentiments which was involved in the presentation of Communism as a way of nation-building for China. Mao Tse-tung's writings before the establishment of the Communist Government had not suggested that there would be any close imitation of the Soviet Union and on the contrary had emphasised that Marxism-Leninism would be "adapted" to conditions in China.

2 Manifesto of 2nd National Congress of CCP, quoted in *A Documentary History of Chinese Communism*, Brandt, Schwartz and Fairbank, George Allen & Unwin Ltd, London, 1952, p. 63.

3 See, for example, *1954 World Atlas* published by Soviet Bureau of Geodesy & Cartography, and map enclosed in *China in Transition*, Peking, 1957.

No public statements were issued about the implementation of the Treaty's provisions for Soviet military support to China but a flow of Soviet military equipment into the country apparently developed during 1950. This military support assumed crucial importance towards the end of the year when the Chinese intervened in the Korean war, but in some respects the experience of dependence on Soviet military assistance must have been a disillusionment to the Chinese. The Chinese forces appeared to lack air cover and military support in Korea, and it was noticeable that after entry into the war the Chinese Communists began to place great emphasis on building up China's economy, which had still been in a process of rehabilitation at the end of 1950.

The pattern of Sino-Soviet co-operation which had been established in 1950 did not change significantly until 1954. Krushchev and a number of Soviet leaders visited Peking for the National Day celebrations in that year and a joint declaration reflected Soviet acceptance of China as an independent and equal state. There were no references to China's recognition of the USSR as the leader of the Communist countries, and relations between China and the Soviet Union were said to be based on the principles of "equality, mutual benefit, mutual respect for national sovereignty and territorial integrity." Proletarian internationalism was not mentioned, and China's acquisition of a more independent status appeared to be emphasised by a notification that the two governments would consult each other in order to achieve "unity of action" in safeguarding their security and maintaining international peace; in addition the declaration indirectly accorded China the status of a "great power."[4] During the Soviet delegation's presence it was agreed to abolish the joint stock companies which had been set up in 1950, and which had evidently been avenues of Soviet economic influence in China; the Soviet Union agreed to hand over Port Arthur Naval Base to China unconditionally by the end of May 1955, although in 1952 the Chinese had assented to an extended stay of Soviet forces at the base until the conclusion of a peace treaty with Japan; finally a new Soviet credit to China of R520 million

4 NCNA, 12 October 1954.

(about US $130 million) was announced, but without any information about the period over which it would be made available.[5]

Of these new arrangements, the first two were probably considered satisfactory by the Chinese, but the size of the new credit may not have been very pleasing. At this stage China was in the second year of her first five-year plan, and there had been several indications that she was seeking additional Soviet economic aid, over and above the US $300 million credit granted in 1950.[6] After the October 1954 economic aid agreement the Chinese must have used considerably stronger leverage against the USSR, for the next aid agreement in April 1956 promised Soviet assistance worth R2500 million, in respect of some 55 new industrial projects, which, according to later information, were to be completed by the end of 1957.[7]

Whatever the real attitude of the Chinese may have been towards the October 1954 aid agreement, it certainly appeared that they were determined to show some independence from the USSR, because Mao Tse-tung, Liu Shao-chi and Chou En-lai did not attend the Peking celebrations of the Soviet October Revolution (6-7 November), and in December 1954 the Sino-Soviet Friendship Association, which had played a prominent part in publicising Soviet achievements in China, appeared to lose official favour.

Tension may have developed in Sino-Soviet relations because of a Soviet move on 11 September to resume diplomatic links with Japan.[8] The Chinese may have foreseen that the USSR would negotiate independently with that country, without exercising pressure on behalf of their interests. At the same time the Chinese may also have detected signs that the USSR intended to develop a campaign of its own for goodwill in India.

The increased independence *vis-à-vis* the USSR which China evidenced in October 1954 was presumably due in a large measure

5 NCNA, 12 October 1954.

6 *Moscow-Peking Axis*, by Boorman and others, Council on Foreign Relations, New York, 1957, p. 88.

7 1959 Economic Planning Report, NCNA, 21 April 1959.

8 James William Morley. *Soviet and Chinese Communist Policies Towards Japan*, Institute of Pacific Relations, 1958, p. 8.

to exploitation of the succession struggle in the Soviet Union, which had begun after the death of Stalin in March 1953. In order to give that independence a broader basis, the Chinese undoubtedly felt obliged to extend and consolidate the prestige and influence which they had acquired in Asia through Chou En-lai's diplomacy towards India and Burma earlier in 1954. A major opportunity to pursue that objective was provided by the Afro-Asian Conference in April 1955. As has been mentioned in Chapter 3, Chou En-lai's efforts at that Conference very much enhanced China's status in South and South-East Asia.

The Soviet authorities, however, apparently decided to challenge the influence which the Chinese were building up in Asia. In mid-1955 the USSR began to negotiate for a restoration of diplomatic relations with Japan, but apparently without attempting to ensure that these negotiations would be of benefit to China.[9] Later in 1955 the Soviet leaders Krushchev and Bulganin visited India, Burma and Afghanistan and gave much prominence to the Soviet Union's wish to provide economic aid to the under-developed countries in Asia—a type of diplomacy in which the Chinese could not compete. Moreover, in their efforts to build up goodwill in India, the Soviet leaders vehemently supported the Indian case concerning the Kashmir dispute, thereby cutting across the successful Chinese diplomacy towards Pakistan which had begun at the Afro-Asian Conference earlier in the year.

Meanwhile the Chinese took advantage of an opportunity to show some indirect opposition to Soviet authority in the Communist system. During 1955 Yugoslavia had opened diplomatic relations with the Chinese Communist government and at her national day celebrations in Peking on 28 November 1955, to which the Chinese gave special prominence, her representatives were congratulated on the success of their country's long struggle for freedom and independence. Similar remarks had been made earlier in the year by Mao Tse-tung when the first Yugoslav Ambassador had presented his credentials, but the national day celebrations were a public occasion and the theme was dwelt

9 Being able to restrict Japanese fishing in waters north of Hokkaido, the USSR was in a position to exert strong pressures on Japan.

upon by the principal Chinese speaker.[10] For the occasion it
was appropriate for the Chinese to show cordiality towards
Yugoslavia, in line with the Soviet Union's endeavours to heal
the breach with her, but by emphasising their sympathy with
the Yugoslav struggle against Soviet domination the Chinese
were presumably intending to assert a degree of opposition to
Soviet authority elsewhere in Eastern Europe

Krushchev's denunciation of Stalin at the Soviet Communist
Party's 20th Congress early in 1956 appeared to stimulate Chinese
ambitions for higher status in the international Communist movement. From this point onwards the course of Sino-Soviet relations
demands close attention. Some developments noted in earlier
chapters will thus be further reviewed.

Domestically, the condemnation of Stalin involved the
Chinese Communist Party in some loss of face, since the Soviet
leader's cult had been promoted in China. Externally, however,
the situation favoured an assertion of some leadership by China
in the international Communist system. This was done by an
article in the *People's Daily,* Peking, on 5 April 1956, entitled
The Historical Experience of the Dictatorship of the Proletariat.
The article praised Stalin for initial fidelity to the "Leninist line"
but indicted him for dictatorial behaviour in his later years and
for "wrong advice" to the international Communist movement.
In order to explain how such "mistakes" could occur in a
"socialist" system, the statement declared that such a system was
not in itself sufficient protection against autocratic behaviour by
its leaders, and that in any "socialist" system it would always
be necessary to struggle against such wrong tendencies in the
higher levels of authority. Responsibilities in a "socialist" system
would have to be shared broadly ("collective leadership") and
a doctrinaire attitude towards the ideology would have to be
avoided.

The Chinese thus implied that Stalin's "mistakes" could occur
again in the USSR or in any other Communist state, and that
China and the East European countries would have to protect
themselves against any future despotic behaviour by the Soviet
authorities. Moreover, the Chinese also implied that the Soviet

10 See NCNA reports of celebrations, 28 November 1955.

71

Union was not entitled to exercise exclusive leadership of the international Communist system.

The Chinese Communist pronouncement produced a situation in which Eastern European Communist movements could be expected to look to China for support against undue Soviet pressures, and this must have contributed to the unrest which developed in Eastern Europe later in the year. Meanwhile, although the Chinese had thus profited at the expense of Soviet prestige and authority, their relations with the USSR had evidently moved on to a more satisfactory basis, presumably on account of their improved leverage, because a new agreement for the provision of Soviet economic aid to China was announced on 7 April 1956—two days after the issue of their doctrinal pronouncement. This new assistance was to be worth R2500 million, as mentioned above.

After these developments the Chinese undoubtedly felt that their international position had become consolidated. Premier Chou En-lai told the National Peoples Congress on 28 June 1956 that China's international status had risen to an "unprecedented" level and that she was playing an ever more important role in determining the course of the whole international situation. Meanwhile there was evidently some satisfaction that China presented a more unified appearance than the Soviet political system. Liu Shao-chi told the 8th Congress of the Chinese Communist Party in September 1956 that the Chinese regime was "the most democratic, the most efficient, and the most consolidated in the history of mankind"; the observation was preceded with the words "like other socialist countries," but in the circumstances it seemed highly probable that the emphasis was intended to be on the qualities of the Chinese regime.

The unrest in Eastern Europe during September 1956 appears to have been initially regarded by the Chinese as a further opportunity to reduce Soviet authority and strengthen China's influence in the international Communist system. When it appeared that the Soviet Union was compromising with the force of nationalism immediately after the Hungarian revolt, the Chinese indicated their support for the independence of the East European regimes, but shortly afterwards, when it became clear that the Soviet Union was determined to crush the Hungarian Revolution, the Chinese gave strong public approval to this Soviet action.[11] Nevertheless, the Chinese continued to show some support for the principle of independence in Eastern Europe, while on the other hand endorsing the Soviet Union's authority over its satellites in this region. This balancing between the principle of independence as between Communist states and the principle of Soviet control was evident in statements made by Premier Chou En-lai during a visit to Poland, Hungary and the USSR in late 1956, and in a Chinese Communist pronouncement of 29 December 1956, which took up again the themes of the April statement on the denigration of Stalin. While in the USSR, Chou En-lai avoided manifesting reservations about Soviet authority over the other Communist countries and this was his attitude in Hungary, but while in Poland he lent some support to the cause of Polish independence. At this time the Poles had succeeded in winning substantial Soviet recognition of their right to conduct their own affairs and the Chinese attitude to this, as reflected in *People's Daily*, Peking, comment on the Soviet-Polish talks of November 1956, was that a Communist country should be recognised as having a large measure of autonomy in its domestic policies, but subject to the overall interests of the international Communist struggle.

The Chinese Communist pronouncement of 29 December 1956, entitled "More on the Historical Experience of the Dictatorship of the Proletariat"[12] was addressed to all Communist states and movements, in the same authoritative tone that had been present in the earlier statement. It declared that the Soviet Union under Stalin had manifested "great nation chauvinism" towards other Communist regimes and parties and it emphasised that the larger Communist countries had to struggle against such tendencies in their dealings with the smaller Communist states— great nation chauvinism would become a "serious danger" in China's foreign policy if precautions were not taken against it. Although it warned against the danger of heavy Soviet domi-

---

11 *Cf.* Chinese Communist comment of 1 November 1956 on initial Soviet statement regarding Hungary, 30 October 1956, and Chinese statements in mid-November 1956 supporting Soviet repression in Hungary.

12 *People's Daily*, Peking, 29 December 1956.

nation in the international Communist movement, however, the Chinese Communist statement affirmed that substantial Soviet authority was necessary to preserve the unity of the Communist regimes and parties. Problems in relations between the USSR and the other Communist countries had to be viewed from the point of view of the movement as a whole, in the interests of "the class struggle on a world scale."

The obligation to accept Soviet leadership was presented in the somewhat disguised form of a requirement to follow the Soviet "path." This path, which in its general form was said to be obligatory for all countries, was defined in terms of basic Soviet experience, viz., acquisition and retention of political power by the Communist Party; socialisation of the country's "culture" and economy; and "dictatorship" over the "landlord and capitalist classes." The imitation of the Soviet Union's example by any particular country could, in the opinion of the Chinese, show some individuality in order to accord better with local characteristics, but these were not to be stretched into a justification for "national" Communism, which would deny the "universal truth of Marxism-Leninism." The Chinese Revolution, although having many "national" characteristics, was nevertheless a "continuation of the Great October Revolution." The "mistakes" of Stalin, although serious, had not affected the validity of the basic features of the Soviet "path."

One of the main purposes of the Chinese Communist statement was to criticize the attitude of the Yugoslavs towards the unrest in Eastern Europe; they were courteously rebuked for "going too far," although some of their criticism of "brother parties" was said to be "reasonable." This restraint was no doubt in line with Soviet policy towards Yugoslavia, for it appeared that the USSR, although it reneged on a promise to Yugoslavia concerning the safety of Hungarian Premier Nagy, was evidently not anxious to cause a wider breach with Yugoslavia. Yet in view of the measured support which the Chinese had been showing for East European and especially Polish demands for autonomy it seemed clear that the degree of respect which they were showing to Yugoslavia was partly intended to raise an additional limit to Soviet authority in Eastern Europe.

Meanwhile an initiative taken by the Chinese outside the context of Soviet-East European relations suggested that they were
prepared to profit from the Soviet Union's difficulties with its
satellites in order to extend further their influence and prestige
in Asia. In addition to visiting the USSR, Poland and Hungary,
Premier Chou En-lai also made an extended tour of South and
South-East Asia, early in 1957, visiting India, Burma, Pakistan,
Cambodia, Nepal, Ceylon and Afghanistan. In each of these
countries he engaged in considerable personal diplomacy of a
quite undoctrinaire character, bringing China's relations with
several of these countries on to a very cordial level. At this time
it would have been quite impossible for any Soviet leader to
engage in such diplomacy towards the non-Communist Asian
countries, owing to the adverse international reactions to Soviet
suppression of the Hungarian revolt.

During the greater part of 1957 the Chinese rather avoided
acknowledging the Soviet Union's authority among the Communist states, but a considerable display of enthusiasm for this
authority occurred at the November 1957 celebrations in honour
of the 40th anniversary of the Soviet October Revolution. These
celebrations were preceded by historic Soviet achievements in
rocketry. After the celebrations the Chinese joined the other
Communist parties of the Soviet bloc in a declaration which
reaffirmed the objective of establishing a world Communist
system in which each Communist regime would follow the
Soviet "path." This was defined in terms similar to those expressed in the Chinese Communist pronouncement of December
1956.

What was presumably the official Chinese Communist comment[13] on this declaration, however, reflected ambitions to
strengthen China's position in the Communist bloc. During the
first half of 1958 the Chinese continued to qualify their endorse-
ment of Soviet authority among the Communist countries by
emphasising the importance of their own international role and
when Krushchev visited Peking at the end of July 1958 Chinese
deference to Soviet leadership disappeared altogether. The
Chinese Communist news services presented China as being in

13 *People's Daily*, Peking, 25 November 1957.

75

partnership rather than subordinate to the Soviet Union and sought to give the impression that Mao Tse-tung's conversations with Krushchev had been responsible for a subsequent change in Soviet diplomacy regarding the crisis in the Middle East,[14] which had developed after the revolt in Iraq. Krushchev's visit took place without any prior notification, and the impression that the Chinese were exerting considerable leverage was heightened by the announcement on 8 August of a new Soviet aid agreement. The value of this aid agreement was not stated, but according to the Soviet notification it was to cover assistance for the construction of 47 industrial projects in China; the Chinese news release did not mention the number of projects and pointedly de-emphasised China's economic dependence on the Soviet Union. The wording of both the Soviet and Chinese announcements was very similar, which suggested that both sides had agreed on a communique and had then used it in different ways.

Soon after the announcement of this new Soviet aid agreement the crisis in the Middle East was resolved and the Chinese made a great show of their determination to seize Taiwan; they seemed to be prepared to carry this through even at the cost of war with the USA. A state of national emergency was proclaimed, and a Chinese bombardment of Quemoy appeared to be preparing the way for an invasion of that island, but it was soon evident that a major objective of the exercise was to produce an atmosphere of crisis within China which would facilitate the rapid merging of the agricultural co-operatives into "communes."

The Chinese claimed that these communes would bring their regime close to "Communism" and this was clearly embarrassing to the Soviet authorities, who at first avoided noting the existence of the communes and later indirectly condemned them. The Chinese, however, persisted in their efforts to establish the communes, although they did modify the claims which they had made about the level of social advancement symbolised by the new organisations. Subsequently, it appeared that the Soviet Union was anxious to make it clear to the rest of the international

---

14 The USSR had at first proposed a Summit meeting within the UN Security Council, at which Nationalist China would presumably have been present.

Communist system that the Chinese had a "vulgar" and "extreme" concept of Communism and were endeavouring to achieve an ideal of equality which could not be reached except after very advanced economic development.[15]

The crisis in the Taiwan Straits, although related to the commune policy, may have been intended also to gain stronger Soviet military support. Early in August, the Chinese had called for unrelenting pressures by the Communist states against the West, but had bitterly criticised certain unidentified sections of the international Communist movement which, through a fear of war, did not wish to press the "imperialists" too hard. This may have been a reflection of Chinese annoyance at the reluctance of the Soviet authorities to become involved in a war over Taiwan: it certainly bore a remarkable resemblance to the more forthright criticisms of the Soviet Union which appeared in 1960. The probability that the Chinese were resenting a lukewarm Soviet attitude regarding Taiwan seemed stronger when an exhibition was held in Peking to display air-to-air missiles which had been given to the Chinese Nationalist Air Force by the USA: the purpose of the display was apparently to emphasise that China had not been able to obtain any similar missiles from the USSR.

Since Krushchev's visit to Peking at the end of July 1958 there had been no acknowledgments by the Chinese of Soviet authority in the international Communist movement, but there was an unexpected return to the recognition of Soviet leadership on 10 December 1958, when the Central Committee of the Chinese Communist Party announced that Mao Tse-tung would not continue as Head of State. Whether there was any connection between these two developments is uncertain, but since Mao Tse-tung had personally encouraged the establishment of the communes it is possible that his removal from office had been demanded by the USSR, although the changes may have been merely a reflection of an internal struggle within the Chinese Communist Party.

There were further endorsements of Soviet leadership over the

15 See article on Transition to Communism by Sobolev, *World Marxist Review*, Vol. III, No. 11, p. 2, and article on Left-Wing Communism by Matkovsky, in *Pravda*, 12 June 1960.

Communist countries in Chou En-lai's speech as head of the Chinese delegation to the 21st Congress of the Soviet Communist Party early in 1959, and the trend towards a more orthodox relationship between the two regimes was further reflected in an announcement on 7 February 1959 concerning a new Soviet aid agreement valued at R5000 million for the period 1959-67. But after this agreement had been publicised the Chinese again began to show reluctance about the acceptance of Soviet authority in the international Communist movement, and at the National People's Congress in April the 1959 Plan disclosed that the 211 major industrial projects which were to have been completed with Soviet assistance in China's first Five-Year Plan (1953-57) had been reduced in number to 166 owing to "mergers in construction" and that of these only 113 had been completed by the end of 1958.[16] This disclosure contrasted sharply with the details of a "great leap forward" achieved in the Chinese economy as a whole during 1958, and it was the first occasion on which the Chinese had given any unfavourable information about the Soviet aid programme.

Meanwhile further tension appeared to be developing in China's relations with the Soviet Union as a result of a divergence of Chinese and Soviet interests in relation to a revolt in Tibet during February and March 1959. The Indian government showed some sympathy with the Tibetan revolutionaries and gave asylum to the Dalai Lama, while permitting numerous expressions of popular sympathy with the Tibetans. This was of no direct consequence to the Soviet Union's diplomacy towards India but it cost the Chinese much prestige, and undoubtedly tended to raise the morale of the resistance movement in Tibet. China showed much hostility towards India, and later there were several border incidents. In September the Chinese indicated that they were claiming large areas of territory from India, east of Bhutan, and in the State of Jammu and Kashmir.

The Soviet Union avoided public comment until 9 September, when it expressed a detached hope that the two countries would settle their misunderstandings.[17] The Soviet Union's real attitude

16 NCNA, 21 April 1959.
17 Tass, 9 September 1959.

towards the Indian government had presumably become hostile during 1958, because of the Indian Congress Party's campaign against the Communist government in the Indian state of Kerala: an attack on Nehru and the Congress Party had been published by a Soviet theorist in the December 1958 issue of *World Marxist Review*. After the Tibetan revolt, however, the Soviet Union presumably decided that support for the Chinese in a demonstration of hostility towards the Indian government would not be a satisfactory way of lightening the pressures on the Indian Communist Party. On the contrary, the USSR emphasised its desire to continue economic co-operation with the Indian government; this prevented the Indian Communist Party from suffering further disgrace, but certain sections of that Party publicly supported the Chinese.

By late 1959 it must have appeared to the Soviet authorities that the Chinese had attached too much importance to venting their illwill towards India. The Chinese on the other hand presumably resented the Soviet Union's lack of solidarity with their position.

Meanwhile Sino-Soviet relations were beginning to be affected by more fundamental complications. In September Krushchev visited the United States in order to prepare the way for a Summit Meeting: the atmosphere of the visit was cordial and the main theme of Krushchev's speeches was the need for "peaceful co-existence," a concept which he handled with much exploitation of its popular significance, and without drawing attention to its esoteric connotation. The Chinese Communist authorities seemed reluctant to notice Krushchev's presence in the USA, and when he arrived in Peking for the National Day celebrations on 1 October he apparently received no public welcome. Moreover, the Chinese Communist news services cut various portions from the speech which Krushchev delivered for that occasion, and in particular a condemnation of "unjust and predatory wars" which he had apparently aimed against the Chinese as a criticism of their attitude on the border question with India. The Chinese also excluded from their reportage of this speech a statement that President Eisenhower understood the need to relax international tension and an assertion that the military superiority of the Communist countries did not justify any policy of aggression against the West.

After Krushchev's departure from Peking there were numerous emphatic Chinese Communist declarations of the need for un-compromising hostility to the West, and during April 1960 a number of articles by Chinese theorists vigorously condemned the idea that there could be "peaceful co-existence" with "the imperialists": imperialism was essentially aggressive and could not be expected to voluntarily undergo any internal change; it had to be opposed resolutely. This belligerent Chinese line was set out in commemoration of the 90th anniversary of the birth of Lenin and was put forward as a faithful application of his doctrine.[18]

Since an East-West Summit Conference was to take place in May, without China's participation, it seemed clear that the Chinese were endeavouring to obstruct Soviet preparations for the Conference, unless it could be assumed that they were work-ing in co-operation with the USSR, in order to give prominence to the threat of global war and thus oblige the West to be more accommodating in its negotiations with the Soviet Union. After Krushchev had refused to participate in a Summit, on the ground that President Eisenhower had not apologised for a reconnais-sance flight by a US aircraft over the Soviet Union, the Chinese presented the episode as proof of their warnings about the West and emphasised that they had not been deceived about the nature of "imperialism." Mao Tse-tung commented on May 14: "Some people have described President Eisenhower as a man who cherished peace. I hope these people will be awakened by the facts." Early in June, Liu Ning-i and Liu Chang-sheng, President and Vice-President respectively of the All China Federation of Trade Unions, reaffirmed in a very outspoken way the impossibility of co-existence with "imperialism." Liu Chang-sheng denied that there was any possibility of the West accept-ing the Soviet Union's proposals for disarmament, and he stated that the Soviet objective in making such proposals was to rouse international public opinion against the "imperialists" so as to isolate them; he ridiculed suggestions that the West would use

18 NCNA, 30 March 1960.

funds saved by disarmament for economic aid to the under-developed countries, citing paraphrased versions of statements which Krushchev had made to the UN General Assembly on 18 September 1959.[19]

Up to this stage the Soviet Union had avoided public criticism of the Chinese line against "peaceful co-existence" with the West, but on 10 and 12 June *Pravda* published the first two of a series of doctrinal attacks on the Chinese position. These indirectly criticised the Chinese as naive left-wing extremists and claimed that fidelity to the spirit of Lenin required much flexibility and patience in revolutionary work so as to permit compromises and co-operation with non-Communist political forces as the occasion demanded. The struggle to promote Communism had to proceed on a sound basis, and the promotion of "peaceful co-existence" with the West was not a "deviation" from Marxism-Leninism, because the struggle for Communism required flexible tactics.

These views were reiterated by Krushchev at a meeting of Communist Parties from the Soviet bloc in Bucharest during June[20] and were further expounded by articles in *Pravda* during August.[21] As against the Chinese, it was held that war could be prevented by the military strength of the Communist countries and that the promotion of "peaceful co-existence" with the West would not be a betrayal of the world revolution because efforts to encourage proletarian seizures of power in the countries out-side the Communist system would continue.

In reply to these Soviet criticisms the Chinese protested that they really desired "peaceful co-existence,"[22] but they also continued with their aggressive line, condemning "revisionists" who feared the destruction of war, and they began to develop their own focus of ideological loyalties by giving an unprecedented status to the "thought of Mao Tse-tung."

The dispute between China and the Soviet Union over strategy towards the West appears to have been discussed at length during the conference of representatives from all sections of the

19 NCNA, 7 and 8 June 1960.
20 *New York Times*, 24 June 1960.
21 *Pravda*, 7, 12 and 26 August 1960.
22 NCNA, 25 and 31 July, 1 August 1960.

international Communist movement in Moscow during November and December 1960. As has been seen in Chapter 4, the Declaration issued after this meeting reflected the Soviet strategy of graduating military and political pressures against the West, but afterwards the Sino-Soviet cleavage remained evident, for the Chinese continued with their own extreme line.

The Moscow conference occasioned a show of Sino-Soviet unity, but relations between China and the USSR had already deteriorated to a point where vindictiveness was becoming apparent on both sides. The Chinese, while persevering with their militant exhortations, had begun to show solidarity with the Albanian Communist regime, whose leaders had been provoking the USSR by opposing Soviet moves for a rapprochement with Yugoslavia.[23] Meanwhile the USSR, in August 1960, had taken the drastic step of withdrawing large numbers of Soviet technicians from China.[24] This undoubtedly dislocated many Chinese industrial plants and it suggested that Soviet assistance to China might be suspended.

Further vindictiveness in Sino-Soviet relations was evident in 1961. In February China injured Soviet prestige in Eastern Europe by promising a credit of R112,500,000 for Albania's economic development, and a later Chinese announcement about this credit implied censure of the USSR by stressing the backwardness of the Albanian economy.[25] Throughout 1961 China herself faced a severe food shortage, which underlined the political motivation of her aid to Albania, but although she publicised her economic difficulties the USSR assisted her only by lending a quantity of sugar and accepting postponement of the exports due from her in 1960.[26]

During the middle months of 1961, however, China and the USSR continued overall co-operation on many international issues, notably those relating to the Congo, Cuba, Laos and Berlin. The Chinese leaders probably resented the USSR's active role in support of the Laotian Communist movement, but that

23 William E. Griffith, *An International Communism?* East Europe, Vol. 10, No. 7, p. 3.
24 Belgrade Radio, 12 August 1960. The Soviet press had hinted that aid to China might be terminated — London *Times,* 31 August 1960.
25 NCNA, 25 April 1961.
26 NCNA, 9 April 1961.

movement's acquisition of control over most of Laos during 1961 was clearly advantageous to China, and China worked in harmony with the USSR at the Geneva Conference on Laos.

Nevertheless, the differences between China and the USSR remained serious and they were exacerbated by the extraordinary events at the 22nd Congress of the Soviet Communist Party in October 1961. The new de-Stalinisation campaign which Premier Krushchev inaugurated at that Congress was aimed not only against his own domestic opposition but also against Albania and, indirectly but more importantly, against China. Faced by this challenge, Premier Chou En-lai, leader of the Chinese delegation, condemned the public criticism of Albania and returned to China while the Congress was still in session. The Chinese news services then displayed much support for Albania, and published Albanian denunciations of Krushchev's attacks.

China and the USSR thus seemed to be on the verge of a complete break. From China's point of view, the situation called for a decisive assertion of her right to contribute prominently to the leadership of international Communism. On the other hand, the USSR was clearly under a compulsion to affirm more effectively its primacy among the Communist states, especially by more vigorous pressures against China. Yet both sides showed restraint, and outwardly their collaboration in the world revolutionary struggle continued. The USSR was no doubt very conscious of its commitments to that struggle, and the Chinese, whose position seemed to be the weaker, may well have decided to observe caution, pending the acquisition of allies, especially in Asia.

CHAPTER 7

Objectives, Strategy and Capabilities

It has been seen that various factors appear to be influencing the development of China's foreign policy along ways which are sometimes complementary and sometimes opposed. China's national interests, understood in a chauvinist-ideological manner, are demanding maintenance of her external security; the utilisation of foreign resources to assist her development into a powerful modern state; and the expansion of China's power and influence, especially into adjacent areas, but by methods consonant with the preservation of her security.

The ideological commitment to contribute to the expansion of Communism calls for support to other Asian Communist movements—and indeed to all sections of the international Communist system—as well as sustained hostility to the "capitalist" countries, especially in order to discourage co-operation with them in Asia. Meanwhile China's commitment to the international Communist movement, and her national interests as her leaders understand them, call for continued alliance with but also competition against the USSR. The weight given to all these factors is evidently determined, to an increasing extent, by the importance of expanding China's international position through exploiting the weaknesses of the South and South-East Asian countries.

The strategies employed in the pursuit of these objectives include protracted struggle against the West and for the expansion of Communism in Asia; the promotion of "peaceful co-existence" in Asia; support for the USSR in the international Communist movement, but also the projection of China as a powerful source of doctrine and guidance for the movement. These strategies are linked together, especially in that "peaceful co-existence" is recommended all the more strongly to other Asian countries by China's struggle against the West and in that the popular diplomacy facilitated by "peaceful co-existence" contributes to the growth of Communism in other Asian countries.

China's capabilities for the implementation of these strategies have become quite strong. Although China lacks the military power which would be necessary in order to face war with the West, she is well placed to provide military support to insurgent Communist struggles in nearby countries, and she can threaten military action against her neighbours as a means of securing their co-operation. Meanwhile she has acquired political influence over some of the Asian Communist movements, and she is able to secure considerable co-operation from the neutral Asian states, other than India.

Objectives

The first external objective of the Chinese Communist regime must be the preservation of its own security. This imposes very important limits on what China can do in order to expand her power. It requires avoidance of the risks of a major war with a modern state, and it calls for the diversion and draining of Western military strength, the exploitation of divisions among the West, and the encouragement of friendly neutrality among other Asian countries. Finally, in the opinion of the Chinese Communist authorities, China's security demands a belligerent attitude towards the West, because firm opposition will discourage the "Imperialists" from aggression.

China's security is listed first among her national interests, but these are understood in the context of an expansionist outlook which is ideological, and, to an increasing extent, chauvinist. The maintenance of China's security is thus something to be undertaken *within* a kind of forward stategy, and this forward strategy itself is considered to play a vital role in the maintenance of her security; the security factor however does mean that in the forward strategy the way must always be left open for a retreat from any belligerent position, so that the regime will not be obliged to face unacceptable risks. Scope for such retreats is provided by much-publicised dedication to "peaceful co-existence."

The second objective in Chinese foreign policy must be the utilisation of external resources in order to assist China's development into a powerful modern state. The ideological context in which this need is understood results in much dependence on the Soviet Union and other Communist countries for supplies of heavy industrial equipment, rather than on utilisation of all the scope for bargaining in the international capital goods market. Although economic assistance is received from the Soviet Union, the regime is evidently not prepared to accept such assistance from the West, except in a disguised way, e.g., through procurements on credit. China's willingness to depend on the other Communist countries for supplies of industrial equipment reflects doctrinal and strategic considerations, but on the other hand China is clearly not willing to integrate her economy with that of the Soviet bloc. Deepening rivalry with the Soviet Union appears to be impelling China to increase somewhat her dependence on capital goods imports from Western Europe but this is presumably subject to limitations on account of China's need to maintain substantial co-operation with the USSR.

The composition of China's foreign trade is of course determined very much by the course of her industrialisation programme; if there is any change towards more investment in agriculture this could result in large imports of farm machinery and chemical fertilisers. Meanwhile the low investment priority for agriculture, which has left that branch of the economy on an insecure basis, results in periodic dependence on imports of grain. If China were to seek more finance for her development by expanding her exports of light industrial products this would require the demonstration of much wider commercial co-operation with the South and South-East Asian countries, and with the West, and politically a much more demonstrative commitment to "peaceful co-existence" would be called for.

The other objectives in China's foreign policy cannot be listed in priorities without some uncertainty. China is evidently endeavouring to expand her power and influence, but largely within and through her efforts to promote Communism abroad. The commitment to the international Communist movement involves hostility to the West and co-operation with the USSR, but the need to strengthen China's status requires competition against the USSR for the loyalty of other sections of the international Communist movement, and for the goodwill of non-Communist Asian governments.

The objective of expanding China's power and influence is evidently intended to be fulfilled through the establishment of satellite Communist governments in the other Asian countries, and possibly further afield. Meanwhile the short-term requirements of security, development and expansion are necessitating much attention to the utilisation of immediate opportunities for influence in the other Asian countries, and hence for compromise with established political forces in those countries. Influenced by the "peaceful co-existence" strategy, there are governments in South and South-East Asia which are committed to foreign policies of non-alignment and which are disposed to accept formal Chinese respect for that non-alignment, especially insofar as this is illustrated by practical forms of economic co-operation. Several such governments are apparently prepared to accede within limits to Chinese demands relating to their domestic and foreign affairs rather than precipitate a drastic switch in Chinese policy towards themselves, which would give them a share in the hostility which China directs towards the West.

Because of the importance of avoiding serious risks to China's external security, the expansion of Communism elsewhere in Asia must presumably go forward by indirect aggression. The vulnerable area of South-East Asia will thus undoubtedly have priority, and all the more so if the Chinese are hoping to recover the political authority which China once exercised in this region. But indirect aggression must evidently be put into effect selectively, so as not to altogether prejudice "peaceful co-existence" in the area as a whole.

The interim pursuit of goodwill in Asia is facilitated by the vigorous hostility which China maintains towards the "imperialists," for this discourages Asian co-operation with the West, gives prominence to China's ascendance in Asia and thus recommends "peaceful co-existence" to the other Asian countries. In recent years, however, China has been placed at a disadvantage by Soviet rivalry in the field of peaceful co-operation, for the Soviet Union has made use of its superior economic power in support of its own diplomacy in Asia. The USSR has provided large-scale economic assistance to several Asian countries and has built up its trade in Asia, although overall this is still well below China's commerce with other Asian countries. As a consequence of this Soviet rivalry, China has evidently been tending to rely more on the encouragement of revolutionary zeal among the Asian Communist movements than on the strategy of "peaceful co-existence" for the expansion of her power in Asia.

The obligation to contribute to the establishment of world Communism requires opposition to "capitalism" and especially towards the leading capitalist country, the USA. To divide the enemy, however, hostility to the lesser capitalist states is restricted, and substantial commercial relations are built up with them. Overall hostility towards the "capitalist" or "imperialist" countries is aimed especially at discouraging Western opposition to advances by other Asian Communist movements. China endeavours to encourage such advances, which, she considers, can be achieved only through armed struggles, and she is committed to support them as much as possible.

The degree to which China can provide military aid to armed struggles by Communist movements in other Asian countries however must be largely conditional on the extent to which the resultant risk of Western intervention will be offset by a firm Soviet deterrent. Hence China has an interest in encouraging Soviet aggressiveness. There are, however, other reasons which must counsel China to encourage vigorous Soviet opposition to the West: any diversion of Western attention and military power elsewhere must tend to improve China's overall security, and meanwhile the more the Soviet Union becomes committed to aggressive strategies towards the West the more difficult it will be for the USSR to switch to conciliatory diplomacy which could prepare for a settlement with the West along lines inimical to China's interests.

The need to assert China's interests as against the USSR must impose additional caution on the Chinese Communist regime about the acceptance of risks of conflict with the West, for it is becoming more and more important for China to decrease her military dependence on the USSR. Hence while China advocates stronger Soviet militancy towards the West she will nevertheless oppose any trend towards her own involvement in war with the West. Her interest in economic co-operation with the lesser Western countries will presumably increase, and if any belligerent position is taken towards the USA the way for a retreat to "peaceful co-existence" must be kept open.

The state of her relations with the USSR will no doubt be the most decisive influence on China's foreign policy. Rivalry between the two regimes will almost certainly increase, because the USSR must seek to curb China's resistance to Soviet authority in the international Communist system, and China's interests are no doubt felt to demand maximum efforts to bring the overall policy of that system as much as possible into line with her needs. A trustful *modus vivendi* between the two powers, based on rational perceptions of self-interest, is most unlikely, for the leaders of each are almost certainly profoundly suspicious of and resentful towards the other, and presumably regard competition against the other for authority in the Communist system as a struggle for total power in which failure could mean severe defeat.

The degree to which the increasing Sino-Soviet rivalry will be restrained by the advantages of co-operation on both sides is difficult to estimate. Further deterioration in Sino-Soviet relations is certainly possible, but China presumably could not face such a prospect because it would oblige her to seek extensive Western economic and indeed military support, which of course might come very slowly. Nevertheless the increasing chauvinist influence in Chinese ideological thinking must make for a more self-reliant, less objective and more impassioned handling of relations with the USSR. Meanwhile, on the Soviet side, although it must be recognised that grave harm would come to the Soviet international position from a decisive break with China, it must also seem desirable to seek a definite solution to the problem of Chinese insubordination before China's independence is further consolidated.

Continuation of the rivalry between China and the USSR on present terms, i.e., with graduated pressures on both sides, will make it important for China to strengthen her international position by expansion in Asia. As her caution about the acceptance of risks of conflict with the West must also be increasing, however, China's foreign policy will presumably be very much influenced by the opportunities for extending her power into neighbouring areas through techniques of indirect aggression. And because her external security requirements must prevent China from extending more than small-scale and unofficial support to projects of indirect aggression in neighbouring areas, she must place emphasis on building up the strength and militancy of the other Asian Communist movements, and consolidating her own influence over them.

Where the degree of co-operation from established Asian governments is substantial, as in the case of Burma and Cambodia early in 1961, the question of supporting revolutionary violence by the local Communist movements can evidently remain in abeyance, especially insofar as this can help to recommend "peaceful co-existence" to other Asian countries. But at the same time success in establishing a Communist regime orientated towards China in one of the South-East Asian countries would be a powerful recommendation for the acceptance or strengthening of "peaceful co-existence" with China by the others—although it might also provoke some of them to align firmly with the West.

Strategy

To promote the expansion of Communism in Asia the Chinese Communist authorities employ in the first place a strategy of *protracted struggle*, which is derived from orthodox Communist doctrine but which has been given current expression by Mao Tse-tung. This strategy is based on a belief in the ultimate success of persistent, cautious and flexible aggression against the "imperialist" countries, who are considered lacking in resolution and courage, and who will therefore always retreat in the face of a resolute threat. This strategy involves confidence in the superior capacity of the Communist movements for ideological and political struggle against the West: in particular the potential for Communist subversion in the non-Communist countries is considered greater than the scope for Western influence in the Communist countries.

The strategy of protracted struggle is put into effect through China's direct opposition to the West and through her support to other Communist parties. For the present she is not engaged in any military conflict with the West but she places great emphasis on maintaining the appearance of resolute determination to use force against the "imperialists." This threat is directed against US military power on Taiwan and is also intended to deter Western intervention against insurgent struggles by Asian Communist movements. China has frequently threatened to invade Taiwan, and has periodically attacked offshore islands held by the Kuomintang.

China endeavours to guide and support the struggles of the Asian Communist movements: those movements are urged to follow the example of persistent armed conflict which led to victory in China, but China's military assistance to their struggles must be restricted, because, for many reasons, it is important for her to avoid involvement in a major war. The Chinese have called for strong militancy by the other Asian Communist movements, but they may be rather less interested than the leaders of those movements in the prospects of success through such struggles. Especially in times of domestic difficulty, the Chinese must be inclined to welcome any revolutionary activities by other Asian Communist movements, however rash from a local point of view, as valuable contributions to the weakening of local anti-Communist forces in Asia, and to the contraction of the Western position. Meanwhile the Chinese may well believe that by committing themselves to difficult armed struggles the other Asian Communist movements will improve their capabilities and gain wider support.

Chinese guidance to revolutionary struggles in South and South-East Asia involves no risk to China's security, but the provision of any Chinese military support to such struggles must proceed on a cautious, unofficial and flexible basis, while the threat of massive Chinese intervention must be employed to dis-

91

courage Western support to target countries in South and South-East Asia, but in a way which will not actually involve China in a major conflict. Protracted struggle through indirect aggression thus means that China's military support to insurgent Asian Communist movements must be limited, disguised and retractable, according to the way in which the danger of Western intervention develops. If no Western intervention appears to be forthcoming China's military support to the insurgents in the target country can be expanded, but if the West does seem likely to intervene, China, after achieving some delay in this threat by threatening massive participation herself, can avoid involvement in a major war by contracting her support to the insurgents, ensuring a reduction of their military activities, and calling for a political settlement, while reiterating her desire for "peaceful co-existence."

Successful protracted struggle through indirect aggression must depend very much on the location of the target country, since the provision of Chinese military support to local Communist insurgents and the projection of a real threat of massive Chinese intervention are feasible only in relation to a country which is adjacent or very near to China. If the country is some distance from China the scope for Chinese participation in a local revolutionary struggle will be very limited, and the possibility of large-scale Chinese assistance to the insurgents will not seem real enough to discourage Western intervention: this appears to be the lesson of Malaya.

Subordinate to the strategy of protracted struggle is the strategy of "peaceful co-existence," which concerns China's relations with the West and with the other Asian countries. *Vis-à-vis* the West this strategy is put into effect by projecting, simultaneously with China's hostility to the "imperialists," her desire for the avoidance of armed conflict with those "imperialists." This is managed by giving a defensive character to China's hostility towards the West, on the ground that the West is always "aggressive": opposition to the aggressors thus amounts to a struggle for peace. To the under-developed countries therefore China does not seem aggressive, her desire to avoid conflict gains some credence in the lesser "imperialist" countries, and the way is kept open for a retreat from any belligerent position which she may take up towards the West. As has been seen, the concept of "peaceful co-existence" has a public relations function distinct from its doctrinal reference to a situation in which the West is deterred from aggression by the superior might of the Communist countries, and is obliged to accept a continual expansion of Communism among the advanced as well as the under-developed countries by methods short of major war.

In relation to the other Asian countries, the strategy of "peaceful co-existence" is put into effect by formal Chinese pledges of dedication to that ideal, but with fairly clear implications that they can enjoy security and China's goodwill only if they avoid co-operation with the West. Initially what is requested of them is simply non-alignment, but once committed to neutrality they are expected to observe that policy in ways favourable to China, so that to an increasing extent "peaceful co-existence" in Asia will be dependent on the co-operation of other Asian countries with China against the West. If a country which has accepted "peaceful co-existence" begins to co-operate substantially with the West it can no longer expect China to be bound by the principles of respect for its independence, etc., which are summed up under the heading of "peaceful co-existence." More importantly, and here the experience of Laos is a useful example, a country which takes active measures against its local Communist movement can stand to lose the benefits of "peaceful co-existence." Finally, a country which has accepted "peaceful co-existence" is intended to be receptive to China's "popular diplomacy": it is expected to tolerate the organisation, by local Communist-front bodies, of a continuous flow of delegations to China, and these are intended to give favourable publicity to Chinese Communism after their return. When a neutral country violates any of these *de facto* conditions of "peaceful co-existence" it may receive, as a warning, a share of the hostility which China directs towards the West.

Apart from the strategy of "peaceful co-existence," but bearing some relationship to the strategy of protracted struggle, is the dual strategy of co-operation with and competition against the USSR. Alliance with the USSR was presumably at first entirely a matter of policy, but it seems evident that with the clear identification of China's interests as separate from those of the USSR—which has apparently occurred since 1953—co-operation with the USSR has become to a significant degree a matter of strategy, although in a large measure continuing to be motivated by ideological commitment. That is to say, although it is still China's policy to work with the USSR for the promotion of world Communism, the form of her co-operation with the USSR is undoubtedly intended to serve China's advancement as an equal partner of the USSR and as a great power with her own pattern of influence among the non-Communist countries. At the same time, while the form of co-operation with the USSR has thus become a matter of strategy, competition against the USSR has also developed.

By taking on the character of strategy, co-operation with the USSR is evidently becoming for China a matter of caution, experiment, and bargaining. The fundamental issues with which this strategy is evidently concerned are the provision of Soviet economic aid to China, and Soviet support for China's expansion in Asia through subversion and indirect aggression. On both these matters China can presumably expect Soviet co-operation proportionate to the manner in which she subserves Soviet interests, but the problem is that two of the main interests of the USSR must be to secure adequate influence over China and to curb the expansion of her power, since otherwise the future of Soviet authority in the international Communist system will not be assured. Because the USSR thus cannot be expected to be very responsive to Chinese co-operation predicated on Soviet reciprocation in economic aid and support for Chinese expansion, China must seek additional leverage against the USSR and must strive to become less dependent on the Soviet Union for economic support and for backing in her expansion. This means that, while endeavouring to become economically self-reliant, China must compete with the USSR for influence over the Asian Communist movements and for the goodwill of Asian governments.

China's competition with the USSR must remain subordinate to her co-operation with the Soviet Union, and as a consequence a great deal of it must probably be disguised. It has certainly become much more public in recent years, however, through the projection of Mao Tse-tung's thought in a way which has given China her own focus of ideological loyalties and presented her as a more dynamic and more "Leninist" example of Communism than the USSR.

Meanwhile, in general, the price of China's competition against the USSR appears to have been, and must be expected to be, a limitation of Soviet assistance for China's development and expansion. China is thus in a situation which obliges her to co-operate substantially with the USSR in order to acquire scope for competition against the Soviet Union, and she may hope to resolve the antithesis between these two strategies by alternating emphasis from one to another. A switch to whole-hearted support for Soviet objectives hitherto lightly regarded may gain China additional Soviet economic aid and perhaps some support for her expansion, and on the basis of her strengthened position she may later be in a better position to assert her interests against the USSR. As has already been indicated, however, the rivalry which has developed between China and the USSR has made it probable that any substantial increase in Soviet support for China's interests will be dependent on a degree of submission to Soviet authority which China would find unacceptable. It is not likely that China will be able to bargain by holding out some special form of co-operation which is urgently needed by the USSR.

Capabilities

The strategy of protracted struggle does not call for sustained full-scale hostilities with the West, which China must avoid because of her lack of nuclear arms, but it demands capabilities for the conduct of local wars and the promotion of indirect aggression, as means of expanding the Communist system and contracting the international position of the West. Such capabilities are being built up in China with the development of large modern conventional forces: at present these forces comprise an army with an estimated strength of about two million men, an air force of some two thousand planes, mostly fighters, and a small navy. These forces are heavily dependent on the USSR for logistic support, and their composition suggests that the USSR has been endeavouring to reserve for itself most of the offensive potential of the Alliance. Hence China must observe caution about involvement in local wars, but there is less need for caution in projects of indirect aggression.

The development of China's armed forces is giving her a capacity to harass the US position on Taiwan in ways which might not provoke retaliation against the mainland, but if such harassment became extensive China would probably be faced with a major conflict. On the Asian mainland, China has the capacity to wage protracted struggles against Western forces in local wars, but in general she cannot accept involvement in such wars if Western strategy indicates that they would develop into major conflicts—and in most local war situations that would probably be the case. Hence it seems clear that China must place great emphasis on developing her capabilities for the promotion of indirect aggression, since this form of struggle involves least risk to her security and is moreover relatively inexpensive.

China's capacity to promote indirect aggression is largely a question of her influence over other Asian Communist movements and of the local potentialities of those movements, but it also depends on the location of the target countries, the likelihood and probable effectiveness of Western intervention, and the expected effects on her international position.

China's influence over the other Asian Communist movements has probably been reduced by the consolidation of Soviet authority over those revolutionary organisations. As has been seen, most of the Asian Communist parties, with the notable exception of the Indonesian Communist movement, apparently supported the USSR against China on the question of strategy towards the West at the November-December 1960 conference of world Communism parties in Moscow. Before that conference, China had complained of "revisionist" restraint on revolutionary struggles in certain unspecified areas and had made it clear that she was calling for strong militancy by the Communist movements in the under-developed countries. Although the Chinese may be meeting significant responses to their revolutionary appeals, they are evidently at a disadvantage in competition with the USSR for the support of other Asian Communist movements because of the breadth of established loyalties to the USSR among those associations, and also because emphasis on the attraction of wider followings rather than on revolutionary action is at present a more fitting strategy for Communist organisations in the several Asian countries which are receiving or being offered Soviet economic aid. This latter point of course has some application in the countries which are receiving Chinese Communist economic aid, but such assistance is relatively small.

In adjacent countries, the proximity of China's power presumably tends to offset Soviet influence over the local Communist movements, since these would certainly be risking their future by supporting the USSR as against China, although once established in power, as the example of North Vietnam has shown, they would undoubtedly find it advisable to attract Soviet interest as a remedy against Chinese pressures.

A further point affecting China's capacity for indirect aggression in South or South-East Asia is the degree of revolutionary potential possessed by those Asian Communist movements which are responsive to her influence. This revolutionary potential may be declining, as, for example, in Burma over the past several years, where the military position of the Burmese Communist Party has been continually weakened by pressure from government forces, or it may be very uncertain, as in the case of the large Indonesian Communist Party. Over the past decade the South and South-East Asian governments have in general improved their abilities to deal with internal disorders. In the immediate future it is unlikely that the Communist parties of those regions will be as favourably placed for insurgent action as they were in 1948 when their countries were endeavouring to gain or consolidate independence from colonial rule. Nevertheless, China has continued to emphasise that they must seek power through revolutionary violence.

The location of a target country must also have an important bearing on China's capacity for indirect aggression against it. Unofficial, flexible and retractable military support can be provided to revolutionary action in an adjacent country much more easily than in one far away, and in relation to a nearby country the threat of massive Chinese participation is a stronger deterrent and delaying force against Western intervention. The strategy of protracted struggle precludes acceptance of Western intervention in response to indirect aggression, and calls instead for acquisition of the gains which can be made short of provoking such intervention. China's capacity for indirect aggression must therefore include scope to contract such a process in order to demonstrate to the West that intervention is not called for, since no further Communist gains are being made: at a later date the process of indirect aggression can be resumed, although it must again be kept short of provoking Western intervention.

For the success of protracted struggle through indirect aggression, therefore, a great deal must depend on China's maintenance of vigorous hostility towards the West. By discouraging or at least delaying any Western decision to intervene China's hostility guarantees an important time period in which indirect aggression can proceed before the local Communist forces contract their activities and switch to the consolidation of their gains, so that Western intervention will be deferred.

The strategy of protracted struggle however does not oblige China to proceed cautiously and experimentally in all her attempts at indirect aggression. The type of indirect aggression outlined above accords well with her military doctrine, but the concept of protracted struggle sanctions rapid gains where these are feasible without prejudice to China's security. Speed in a project of indirect aggression will in itself be a guarantee against Western intervention, and this guarantee will be stronger if such aggression is disguised in motive, on the one hand, and popularly supported on the other.

The Chinese may well be considering the advantage of this alternative approach, but in order to put it into effect fully they may have to be prepared to work with non-Communist dissident forces in the target countries. A rapid seizure of political power in another Asian country will usually be within the capabilities only of discontented elements within the established elite, especially among the leaders of the armed forces; such elements however are more likely to have a neutralist rather than a Communist outlook. Indirect aggression along these lines is probably considered to be especially appropriate against the Asian countries which have aligned themselves with the West, but it may also be considered applicable to any non-aligned country whose neutrality has taken an unfavourable trend.

A final determinant of China's capacity for indirect aggression in Asia is the likely pattern of consequences to her international position. If China could anticipate strong Soviet opposition to a particular project of indirect aggression—e.g., against a government which had been responding to Soviet diplomacy—she would then have to assess whether the likely gains of such indirect aggression would be worth the strain in her relations with the USSR. Meanwhile China presumably cannot take up an attitude that is too openly belligerent *vis-à-vis* a target country because this could well cause other Asian states to co-operate actively with the West: her belligerence must continue to be directed largely against the "imperialists." China, moreover, evidently must avoid precipitating indirect aggression in more than one location at a time, because of the likelihood of very unfavourable reactions elsewhere in Asia, and the increased danger of Western intervention. Lastly, China has to take into account the possibility that an Asian government which survives a threat of indirect aggression may afterwards align itself with the West.

China's capabilities to conduct her strategy of "peaceful co-existence" in relation to the West appear to be conditional on the reiteration of her *desire* for peaceful relations with the Western powers, which are projected in the course of her denunciations of the "imperialists," but the strategy is also dependent on her sustained hostility to the West and on her ability to convince the West that her objectives are limited. The joint effect of these factors is to provide China with a way of retreat from any belligerent position taken towards the West, particularly in relation to projects of indirect aggression in Asia. Meanwhile the strategy of "peaceful co-existence" as directed towards the West is also dependent on China's exploitation of divisions among the "imperialists," especially through substantial commerce with the lesser Western countries.

As directed towards other Asian states, the strategy of "peaceful co-existence" requires effective Chinese diplomacy to hold out the prospect of genuine respect for their independence subject only to their non-alignment with the West. Also necessary however is a projection of China's military power, together with demonstrations of her hostility towards the West, so as to give urgency to the question of "peaceful co-existence." A great deal must still depend, of course, on the credibility of the "peaceful co-existence" diplomacy, and in this respect China's capabilities have been reduced since 1959 because of her behaviour towards India, the first country which accepted her pledges of "peaceful co-existence." Nevertheless, China's rather belligerent attitude towards India has caused the small nearby neutral states to become more susceptible to her pressures on questions of co-operation which she may in effect designate as conditions for continued respect of their non-alignment. States which have accepted "peaceful co-existence" with China will tend to be compliant where the matter in question seems to be a small evil in comparison with the implied threat of Chinese displeasure. China, however, must be careful to graduate her demands on countries which have accepted "peaceful co-existence," otherwise the reactions may be very unfavourable. It must be observed, too, that China's capabilities in this context have been seriously reduced by Soviet rivalry for the goodwill of several other Asian states: those states have thereby acquired scope to resist Chinese pressures while courting the favour of the Soviet Union.

China's capabilities for economic diplomacy in support of her "peaceful co-existence" strategy in Asia are quite limited, but they are significant in her relations with the smaller Asian states. China's commerce with the other Asian countries is a relatively unimportant factor in their foreign trade, except in the case of Ceylon; some years ago it became very important for Burma, but this lasted for only a short period. The direction of Chinese economic development implies only slow increases in China's imports of primary products from South and South-East Asia, and in China's exports of light industrial items to those regions; meanwhile few exports of capital goods from China can be expected.

China has provided economic assistance to some of the smaller

Asian countries, notably Cambodia, Nepal and Ceylon, but the value of this assistance has been quite limited, and China cannot expand this assistance without sacrificing some of her own industrial and agricultural development. In the foreseeable future it is unlikely that she will be able to compete with either the USSR or the USA in the provision of economic aid to the other Asian countries. But if China were to concentrate her limited resources for economic diplomacy against one of the smaller Asian countries—purchasing much of its produce and providing it with substantial economic assistance—the result could be a very effective fulfilment of the "peaceful co-existence" strategy. China would presumably acquire very strong influence over the government of that country, for it would be prepared to acquiesce in Chinese requests over a fairly wide range of affairs rather than face the loss of the Chinese market and a withdrawal of Chinese economic assistance. Partial attempts at this kind of concentrated economic diplomacy have been made in relation to Burma and Ceylon, but these two examples have shown that the Chinese must also take into account the likelihood of unfavourable reactions. After 1955, Burma found it advisable to reduce her dependence on trade with China, while Ceylon, although remaining significantly dependent on China's rubber purchases, has in recent years become less susceptible to China's economic influence. Since 1957 China's imports from her have been reduced and the prospect of favourable balances for Ceylon, as were customary under previous trading arrangements, has been eliminated.

The dual strategy of co-operation with and competition against the USSR must call for a very wide range of Chinese capabilities. It seems clear that China could increase her co-operation with the USSR and that she is therefore in a position to bargain extensively with the Soviet Union, up to the point of risking graver strain in the Alliance. At present the USSR apparently enjoys no concessions in China regarding the exploitation of natural resources or the use of bases, ports or communications. The Chinese leaders would presumably consider it inadvisable to allow the USSR any such concessions, but they might be tempted to do so in exchange for greater Soviet assistance in their industrialisation, or Soviet acceptance of a wide zone of influence for them in Asia.

Meanwhile, in order to gain favour with the USSR, China could discontinue her communes and revert to her previous form of collectivised agriculture, thus ending her controversial departure from the Soviet model. China could also discontinue the cult of Mao Tse-tung, which is an embarrassment to the USSR, especially as he is presented as the leading theorist of the international Communist movement. Moreover, China could cease dissenting from Soviet doctrine and strategy towards the West, and she could show full acceptance of Soviet authority over the regimes in Eastern Europe; finally she could discontinue her pressures against India in relation to the border disputes, thus removing a serious impediment to Soviet diplomacy towards India.

All these matters, however, with the exception of the ones relating to the communes and perhaps also the question of relations with India, are important elements in the consolidation of China's independence from and equality with the USSR: it is not feasible for China to give way on any of these points in order to further her interests as a great power. What China can concede is presumably no more than a temporary reduction of emphasis on some of these points, with the proviso that this will be made up later after she has gained the advantage expected from her concession. Such a manoeuvre appears to have been attempted several times through China's alternating acceptance of Soviet leadership in the Communist bloc between 1956 and 1959. But with the development of China's independent stature compromises on questions vital to her great-power status must become less and less feasible, and all the more so because of domestic factors mobilised in support of that status: insofar as loyalties in the Chinese Communist Party have been rallied for the assertion of that status, a reversion to demonstrative approval of Soviet authority in the international Communist system becomes virtually impossible.

China's competition against the USSR requires different capabilities according to the way it concerns the leadership of the Communist states and movements, strategy towards the West or scope for influence among the non-Communist Asian countries. China has no capacity to compete with the USSR for the leadership of the East European states, for although it was possible for her to support the cause of East European independence up to certain limits in 1956 the situation has changed greatly as a result of her extreme measures in domestic and foreign affairs since 1958. The East European countries now have strong reason to support the present Soviet leadership as against China, for central authority based on the Chinese position would impose on them much stricter subordination in order to ensure their fidelity to the more extreme form of Communism expounded by China. Albania must be regarded as an exception, but her case is evidently more a matter of resistance to Soviet authority, and to any Soviet rapprochement with Yugoslavia, than of commitment to China's leadership of the Communist system.

China has some capacity to compete with the USSR for influence over the other Asian Communist states, because of her more dynamic approach, but here again the more exacting subordination implied by her extreme lines on domestic and foreign affairs would be an obstacle to the consolidation of any goodwill among such states. It has already been seen that China is at a serious disadvantage in competing with the USSR for leadership over the Asian Communist movements, except in adjacent countries. Any wavering movement must be strongly influenced by the extent to which support for Soviet authority is already established in the international Communist system as a whole and among the other Asian Communist Parties: it must also be strongly influenced by the superior position of the USSR as compared with China in economic diplomacy towards the non-Communist Asian governments.

China cannot compete effectively with the USSR in setting strategy towards the West for the other Communist states and movements, but she can exercise much leverage against the Soviet Union in relation to that strategy. Her main capabilities in this connection are to take either a more extreme or a softer line in her own diplomacy towards the West. In recent years the first alternative has been in evidence, and China is clearly capable of sustaining this approach. China cannot oblige the

Soviet Union to discontinue its own strategy but by obstructing that strategy she may procure some modifications of it, especially in order to obtain more consideration for her interests. China has a capability to encourage dissent from Soviet strategy among the other Communist movements by the use of her ideological influence, and although this may not seriously threaten overall Soviet authority in the international Communist system it must be an important form of pressure against the USSR. Use of this capability however must no doubt be restricted because continued co-operation with the USSR is still of fundamental importance to China.

China could take a softer line than the USSR towards the West, although in principle short of precipitating more dangerous strain in her relations with the Soviet Union. She would have to anticipate strong Soviet pressures against her change in policy, especially through the withholding of economic support. In such a situation China would be obliged to expand very much her commerce with the West and perhaps to seek Western capital goods on credit. Through following softer diplomacy towards the West however China would reduce the projection of her great-power status in Asia, and her influence over other Asian states would tend to weaken, because those states would see less risk in incurring her displeasure.

It has been noted that China's ability to compete against the USSR for influence over the non-Communist Asian countries is inferior because of the Soviet Union's powerful international position and especially its greater capacity for economic diplomacy. In relation to small adjacent countries, however, the proximity of Chinese military power must offset the advantages possessed by the USSR, although the governments of such countries may be able to improve their position as against China by attracting Soviet attention. The presence of local Communist parties in nearby countries means that their governments are threatened by the possibility of active unofficial Chinese support to those movements, and if they have accepted "peaceful co-existence" with China they must be inclined to hope that by favourable co-operation with her in their foreign affairs they will defer the threat of Chinese assistance to revolutionary action by their national Communist movements. At the same time, fear of China's displeasure must tend to inhibit actions against those Communist organisations. China is thus in a position to exercise influence over the governments in small adjacent countries, while perpetuating subversive threats to their stability.

China's capabilities to manage co-operation with and competition against the USSR must be utilised in a way which gives overall priority to the continuation of the Alliance on a reasonably effective level; but her capabilities for asserting her interests as against the USSR are being further developed, and what is probably more important her chauvinism is becoming more pronounced. This chauvinism combined with what appears to be an intensely "sectarian" and doctrinaire commitment to her side of the ideological dispute with the Soviet Union probably tends to result in a certain blindness to the practical advantages of sustained co-operation with the Soviet Union.

CHAPTER 8

Challenges to Asia and the West

As an ally and also as a rival of the Soviet Union in the struggle for the promotion of World Communism, China presents challenges to the other Asian countries and to the West. Grave dangers are presented to South-East Asia especially because of this region's vulnerability to indirect aggression. With these dangers go strong influences encouraging neutrality among the South-East Asian allies of the West.

Although it seems evident that China is endeavouring to avoid involvement in a major war, and will continue to do so for at least the next decade, she is developing strong capabilities for direct aggression against her Asian neighbours. Nevertheless it seems probable that the factors encouraging emphasis on expansion through *indirect* aggression will continue to dominate her foreign policy.

Indirect aggression is a strategy which offers cumulative limited gains in the expansion of Communism with low risks to China's security, low demands on her resources, and minimum prejudice to her international position — especially in relation to those countries which in varying degrees are co-existing peacefully with her and limiting their co-operation with the West. China is capable of indirect aggression against other Asian countries because of her influence over their Communist movements, although that influence must be shared with or maintained in competition against the USSR. Insurgent action undertaken by such movements can be given unofficial military aid from China, according to geographical and political circumstances. As has been seen, the scope for such assistance is widest in areas adjacent to China, in relation to which China is best able to discourage Western intervention by threatening massive participation on behalf of Communist insurgents.

The extensive publicity work for Communism which China

directs towards all other Asian countries prepares the way for indirect aggression. China presents Communism as the true path of nation-building for the underdeveloped areas, and emphasises that this is also the way to consolidated independence from "imperialism." Both themes receive added weight from China's projection of herself as the strong power of Asia and as a resolute and successful opponent of the West. As a way of nation-building, Communism also receives some recommendation from China's diplomacy of "peaceful co-existence," for this diplomacy deflects attention from the expansionist aspects of Communism and implies sustained Chinese respect for the independence of other Asian countries.

The continued development of China's war potential increases the threat of massive participation with which she can discourage Western intervention against insurgent action by Communist movements under her patronage in neighbouring areas. This threat will become much more serious when China acquires nuclear weapons; these will add directly to the threat, and they will decrease her caution about the dangers of conflict with the West. Meanwhile, the building up of China's war potential also increases the threat of *direct* aggression which she poses against the non-Communist Asian countries. The rates of military advance in those countries are much slower than China's, and it goes without saying that if their security is to be maintained the growing magnitude of her direct military threat will have to be offset by advances in the power of the Western deterrent. Meanwhile, as China's military challenge becomes more prominent in Asia, her scope for exercising pressures against her neighbours will increase, and she will be able to recommend "peaceful co-existence" to them more strongly, while calling on them to join her opposition to "imperialism."

China's intentions and capabilities make it urgent for the non-Communist Asian countries to overcome their vulnerabilities to indirect aggression and to improve their strategic positions. In both respects, increased co-operation by these nations with each other is demanded. Their basic weaknesses can best be remedied by collective regional efforts, in the direction of economic and political integration.

The Asian neutrals are vulnerable to China's pressures because of their lack of solidarity with each other and because they are reluctant to have recourse to the West. They are inclined to avoid actions unfavourable to China, because they do not wish to face a show of her hostility which could threaten to entangle them in her struggle against "imperialism" and thus force them out of their non-alignment. China has made it clear that she expects them to favour the international Communist struggle against "imperialism": this obligation is considered to follow from their desires for "peaceful co-existence." But China has clearly recognised that she can anticipate only limited co-operation from the neutral Asian countries; she can expect them to compromise on questions which they will regard as being of less consequence than the difficulties and dangers which they would have to face if she became hostile, but she cannot allow her attitude to appear too demanding, otherwise their reactions could be very unfavourable. The prospects of "peaceful co-existence" for those countries must be kept sufficiently real. Yet because of her basic interest in probing and exploiting their dispositions to compromise it appears that China's attitude towards them constantly tends to become overbearing.

Most of the West's Asian allies are in varying degrees receptive to China's diplomacy of "peaceful co-existence" and to her publicity activities on behalf of Communism; at the same time some of them are vulnerable to direct Chinese aggression and/or Chinese supported revolutionary action by their local Communist parties. For them, accommodation with China must seem advisable whenever there is any manifest weakening in the military support which they receive from the West.

In order to expand Communism — and her own power — China endeavours to remove Western influence, assistance and protection from Asia. In particular she endeavours to discourage Far Eastern and South-East Asian countries from accepting or continuing co-operation with the United States, and at the same time she seeks to promote tensions between the United States and its major Western allies, towards whose restricted interests in Asia she can afford to be indulgent.

The scale, direction and intensity of the challenges presented by China must vary according to her relations with the USSR, the positions and policies of the West, and the opportunities which she sees for the promotion of Communism in Asia. A major determinant of her policy is undoubtedly the importance of utilizing as soon as possible the scope for Communist expansion through indirect aggression in South-East Asia, before that region's vulnerabilities are significantly reduced by Western assistance and local progress, and also before it is further penetrated by Soviet influence.

Asian Responses

The responses of the non-Communist Asian countries to the challenges presented by China have varied between close co-operation with the West and pro-Communist neutrality. Almost all the non-Communist Asian countries have been influenced in one way or another by hopes of avoiding entanglement in China's struggle against "imperialism," and for this reason China has endeavoured to demonstrate to her neighbours that her basic conflict is against the West and in particular against the USA on account of its "interference" in her internal affairs through "occupation" of Taiwan. This has been intended to convince other Asian countries that alignment with the USA against the danger of Communist expansion in Asia would involve complicity in the USA's "aggression" against China. The neutral Asian countries have thus been encouraged to persevere in their non-alignment, and the Asian allies of the West have been in some respects dissuaded from provoking China and have tended to view their commitments to the Western alliance system exclusively in the light of their own immediate external security problems. Several of those allies have shared the doubts about the reliability of the West which have influenced their neutral neighbours, and meanwhile many of them have been dissatisfied at not receiving preferential Western economic aid, expecting such reciprocation in view of the dangers which they have accepted in co-operating with the West.

The Asian countries which had chosen neutral foreign policies before the formation of SEATO in 1954, viz., India, Indonesia, Burma and Ceylon, responded favourably to China's "peaceful co-existence" campaign between 1954 and 1959, and they were joined by Cambodia after 1955. The "peaceful co-existence" diplomacy also produced favourable reactions for some time in Laos and it tended to weaken the commitments of Thailand and Pakistan to SEATO. This diplomacy was supported by Chinese efforts to build up trade with other Asian countries and by the development of a small but significant Chinese foreign aid programme.

The neutral Asian countries, by accepting "peaceful co-existence," enabled China to engage in "popular diplomacy" and thereby Communism gained considerable approval among their peoples as a way of nation-building. In this process, reports of China's economic attainments played an important role. Meanwhile, China found ways to publicise Communism in some of the Asian countries which were allied to the West, and as a way of nation-building it had a considerable impact among their peoples also.

In general, China's presentation of Communism as the ideal path of development has answered serious dissatisfaction in the South and South-East Asian countries about the slow rates of industrial and agricultural advancement achieved under politico-economic systems which have placed emphasis on the initiative of Western-style private enterprise. Communism has held out prospects of more rapid economic advancement than that possible by imitation of the West, and has thus offered a restoration of prestige to the Asian peoples who have felt humiliated by their failure to emulate Western material progress after liberation from colonial rule. Communism has also appeared to promise effective mobilisation and direction of the national energies which have been dissipated by the factionalism, disloyalties, corruption and inefficiency persisting in the authoritarian as well as the democratic Asian states. Moreover, this ideology has guaranteed to put an end to all the uncertainties and disputes about the correct path of economic and social advancement which have helped to paralyse co-operation for development in the South and South-East Asian countries. Finally, Communism's ostensible emphasis on social justice has answered to disapproval of the exploitation which appears to be endemic to economic systems such as those which have developed in Asia under Western influence.

In projecting the nation-building appeal of Communism, China, because of her backwardness, has lagged behind the USSR, and she has not been well placed to provide economic assistance on an extensive scale to her neighbours. But precisely because of the vigorous efforts which she has been making to achieve rapid development her attainments have evoked admiration elsewhere in Asia, and this has cut across antipathies to Communism as a political system.

China's projection of the nation-building appeal of Communism has made a wide impact in Japan, notwithstanding that country's level of industrial development and its relatively high living standards. Although there have been no diplomatic relations between the two countries, Japanese governments have permitted very extensive unofficial contacts with the Chinese Communist regime. To a considerable proportion of Japan's politically-conscious public opinion, China's example in nation-building has seemed highly recommendable because their own country's advances in recent years, although rapid, have involved the continuation of grave injustices; in addition the Chinese example has been felt to reflect a more noble approach to the work of national development than Japan's own imitation of Western capitalism.

The favourable publicity which Communism has received in Japan as a result of China's initiatives has nevertheless been of little direct benefit to the Japanese Communist Party, which has remained a very small force. That publicity instead appears to have contributed to the development of broader support for the Japanese Socialist Party, an extreme left body which favours neutrality and close co-operation with China and the Soviet Union. The Socialist Party forms the principal opposition to the ruling conservative Liberal-Democratic Party but it has not had sufficient strength to compete equally against the Liberal Democrats, and some of its gains have been offset in recent years by the loss of its right wing, which has formed a separate political organisation, the Democratic Socialist Party.

Among the *under-developed* Asian countries, India has been in the best position to compete against China's projection of the nation-building appeal of Communism. With extensive Western and some Soviet assistance, India has been endeavouring to build up rapidly an advanced economy with a large public sector. Her net domestic investment, however, is considered to be about 11% of her national income as compared with something approaching 20% for China; her agricultural production has been well below her requirements, and her industrial advances have been very much less than China's. Realisation of the slow pace of her economic advancement, together with disappointment at the shortcomings of the ruling Congress Party, have caused a considerable proportion of India's intelligentsia, students, and workers to look to Communism as a more certain, swifter and more effective way of development, notwithstanding its harsh regimentation. In particular such people have felt that only drastic Communist methods of social mobilisation would enable India to overcome the backwardness of her agriculture.

The publicising of China's achievements in India was facilitated by the cordial relationship of "peaceful co-existence" which existed between the two countries from 1954 until 1959. Within that relationship China was able to direct much popular diplomacy towards India, and she received co-operation from organisations set up by the Indian Communist Party for the promotion of Sino-Indian friendship. Meanwhile, the Indian Government made few attempts to explicitly counter the nation-building appeal of Communism or to rally public opinion behind its own efforts to develop the country. But after 1959 the breach with China produced an unfavourable atmosphere for advocacy of the nation-building potential of Communism in India, and it appeared to promote stronger national unity within the country, while contributing to some increase of public support for the Congress Party, notwithstanding continued evidence of corruption and factionalism within that body.

Of the other under-developed Asian countries, Malaya and the Philippines, and to a lesser extent Thailand and Pakistan, have been making some economic progress, but below the rate needed for self-sustained growth. The Chinese Communist Government has not succeeded in promoting "peaceful co-existence" with these states. Pakistan, however, has maintained official relations with the Chinese Communist Government and the cordiality of those relations has in effect enabled China's popular diplomacy to exercise considerable influence on Pakistani public opinion.

Thailand and Malaya have avoided establishing official relations with the Chinese Communist Government, but publications and films from the China mainland have entered both countries in large numbers, and have exercised much influence, particularly among the local Chinese. China, however, has had little opportunity to engage in publicity activities in the Philippines, because the Philippine Government, in addition to following a non-recognition strategy, has vigorously prevented the development of unofficial contacts with the Chinese Communist regime.

Living standards in Malaya and the Philippines have been relatively high but the governments of those countries have exerted little leadership in nation-building and in the promotion of social justice, and have left the greater part of their national development to the initiative of local and foreign private enterprise. Such enterprise has made notable advances, but overall development has not been sufficient to attain self-sustaining growth, and if this deficiency is to be made up within a reasonable time the public sectors of those economies will undoubtedly have to be expanded, especially for the provision of adequate social overhead capital.

In Thailand and Pakistan there has been a similar although less marked reliance on unco-ordinated private enterprise as the main factor in economic development. Some leadership in nation-building has been exercised by the authoritarian military administrations in these two countries, but without any doctrine of economic advancement, with only a modest mobilisation of their countries' resources and without the co-operation of any active political movements. On the other hand, there have been substantial opportunities for popular participation in government under the Malayan and Filipino political systems, yet in both cases there has been a serious lack of public confidence in the dedication of the leading political parties of those countries to the work of nation-building.

More rapid economic development may occur in Malaya, the Philippines and Thailand through co-operation with each other

113

in the building up of commerce and industry within the new Association of South-East Asian States. This Association may make progress in the direction of a common market, while promoting specialisation in industrial development among its members. Other South-East Asian countries, however, appear to be with-holding their support from the Association until they have evid-ence of its success, and meanwhile some of them, notably Burma, have apparently been discouraged by Chinese Communist hos-tility towards the Association on the ground that it represents an extension of SEATO.

Economic development has been seriously retarded in Burma and Indonesia over the past decade, owing to protracted internal strife, political instability, and extensive maladministration. Con-sequently these countries have been fairly receptive to China's presentation of the nation-building potential of Communism. In Indonesia this has contributed to large increases in popular sup-port for the Communist movement, but, in Burma, China's publicity activities have proceeded in less favourable circum-stances, because of the Burmese Communist Party's long-standing armed struggle against the Government, and popular awareness of Chinese Communist military pressures along the north-eastern border. China has been able to maintain "peaceful co-existence" with Burma by de-emphasising her sympathy with the insurgent Burmese Communist Party, but the military danger which she presents has evidently assumed more prominence because of Burma's exposed position since the deterioration of Sino-Indian relations. Before that deterioration Burma's external security had received some support from India's interest in the protection of her own north-eastern territory, but since 1959 India's rather defensive attitude towards China has implied some weakening in Burma's strategic position.

In Indonesia the projection of Communism as a way of nation-building proceeded on a favourable basis between 1954 and 1959 because of the maintenance of unstrained "peaceful co-existence" with China and the rather privileged position which the Indonesian Communist Party acquired through the more or less open patronage of President Soekarno. The Indonesian Com-munist movement itself was energetic in the cultivation of public support and its discipline was able to recommend the Party as a body capable of leading the country out of the indecision and weaknesses resulting from a proliferation of political organisations. President Soekarno's gradual introduction of a "guided democracy" provided more favourable conditions for an extension and consolidation of the Party's influence. Since 1959, however, the strain in Indonesia's relations with the Chinese Communist Government over questions relating to the local Chinese has had an adverse effect on Communist publicity work in Indonesia, and meanwhile the Communist movement's position has been made difficult by opposition from some of the country's military leaders, who have imposed restrictions on its activities.

The varying degrees to which China has succeeded in encouraging support for Communism among the South-East Asian countries have increased their vulnerability to local revolutionary action. Important sections of public opinion in several South-East Asian countries have tended to give approval to Communism as the solution for their country's problems, and potential opposition in such countries to future Communist struggles for power has been reduced.

Most of the South and South-East Asian states are vulnerable to insurgent Communist action because of their predominantly agrarian character, their lack of cultural unity, and the absence of strong ties between their small ruling elites and their socially-fragmented peasant masses. Some of those vulnerabilities are being overcome through economic advances, wider education, and improvements in the armed forces and in the internal security systems, but as has already been pointed out the building up of political unity in support of national development in most of these states is lagging seriously. In several cases, the emergence of leaderships capable of rallying public loyalties for the work of nation-building is being hampered by the continuation in power of corrupt and ineffective elites and by multiple divisions of principle and allegiance at all levels of political authority.

Among the *neutral* Asian states, only Burma has been faced with serious revolutionary violence by its local Communist Party and thus far Chinese Communist assistance to that organisation appears to have been very restricted. The threat from that movement has in fact declined as a result of effective Government counter-action. The other neutral Asian states showed little concern at the danger of Communist insurgence in Burma even when this threat was very grave, however, and they, together with Burma, have since exhibited little solidarity with the other Asian countries which have been threatened in this way. But over the past several years, the Indian, Burmese and Indonesian Governments have placed increasing emphasis on the improvement of their own internal security.

India was threatened by insurgent Communist action soon after gaining independence but this was a relatively small problem and the danger had been virtually eliminated by 1951. Since then, the Indian Communist Party has concentrated on political methods of strengthening its position and this has been in accord with the Party's role as a kind of loyal opposition since 1955, as a consequence of the Government's receipt of economic aid from the Soviet Union.

A revolt by the Indonesian Communist Party in 1948 was overcome quickly by military action which eliminated many of the Party's leaders and seriously reduced its strength. Several years were needed to recover from this defeat, but the Party then found itself able to build up large scale public support, especially after the introduction of China's "peaceful co-existence" diplomacy in 1954. Subsequently, Indonesia's acceptance of Soviet economic aid counselled further reliance on political methods of improving the Party's position, and such methods became even more advisable in the favourable circumstances of "guided democracy" as these evolved after 1958. Nevertheless, the Indonesian Communist Party had been receptive to Chinese Communist influence and this suggests that it has been in sympathy with China's emphasis on armed struggle by Communist movements in the under-developed countries.

Of the Asian SEATO members, only the Philippines has been threatened by Communist insurgent action, and that danger has been greatly reduced in recent years as a result of vigorous military and social measures introduced under the late President Magsaysay. The Philippines and Thailand have meanwhile been very sensitive to the dangers of Chinese and North Vietnamese-

116

supported Communist insurgence in Laos, and they have been disillusioned by the reluctance of the Western SEATO powers, especially Britain and France, to meet the challenge of indirect aggression in that country. As a result, Thailand has given some indications of moving towards a neutral foreign policy, while the Philippines has evidently become hostile to the British and French roles in SEATO. Meanwhile Pakistan's attitude towards the dangers of indirect aggression in South-East Asia has apparently become more detached.

In general the non-Communist Asian countries have exhibited tendencies to evade the *direct* military challenge from China. This challenge has not been explicitly recognised by the neutral Asian states, although their actual awareness of this threat has contributed very much to their non-alignment, and that non-alignment has reflected hopes of inducing the Chinese to direct the threat elsewhere. The neutrality of these countries has even excluded the formation of solidarity with each other, due on the one hand to India's reluctance to exercise the leadership which she had begun to acquire in South and South-East Asia, and, on the other hand, to their individual fears of drawing Chinese hostility through merging in a neutral bloc.

For the neutral Asian countries, the question of response to China's threat of direct aggression in the Far East or in South-East Asia has of course been bound up with the question of co-operation with the major Western powers: they have viewed this latter question unfavourably because of their suspicions of Western "imperialism" and because they have been reluctant to accept the inferior status which has been inevitable for Asian countries entering the Western alliance system. Meanwhile, they have had some expectations of reducing China's aggressiveness by avoiding actions which would provoke her.

The Chinese military challenge to India has been immediately linked with claims to sovereignty over large border territories, but beyond the short term it has implied the development of a threat that would assist the expansion of Communism in India, e.g., through the provision of support to insurgent action by the Indian Communist Party, after subversion and infiltration in frontier areas. The Indian Government has affirmed its determination to resist any Chinese advances but has also indicated that it will not attempt to recover by force the territory occupied by the Chinese up to late 1959. China's military challenge has not as yet disposed India to regard her external security as being bound up with successful resistance to Chinese military challenges elsewhere in Asia, and India has evidently felt unable to sustain a strategy of broad opposition to the Chinese Communist regime. At the same time India has apparently seen some hope of securing Soviet restraints on China's aggressiveness and to that end has continued cordial relations with the Soviet Union, especially by responding to Soviet initiatives for increased mutual economic co-operation.

Apart from the small states on India's northern border, Burma has been more exposed than the other neutral countries to Chinese Communist military pressures. In 1956 Chinese forces occupied frontier areas in Burma across what was called the 1941 boundary line, although it had been agreed in 1954 that the two countries would settle the delineation of the boundary through diplomatic channels. After the 1956 incursion the Chinese Communist forces were soon withdrawn, in accordance with a tentative arrangement, but the Chinese Communist Government did not agree to a final settlement until January 1960, by which time it had become clear that such a move would carry special advantages in relation to China's border dispute with India. This final settlement was somewhat more generous to Burma than the earlier arrangement, thereby giving evidence of China's willingness to compromise in disputes with her neighbours. Moreover, this settlement involved acceptance of a boundary which represented a continuation of the frontier which India was endeavouring to maintain east of Bhutan, and it thus implied that the Chinese were ready to abandon their claims to India's north-east border areas: later the Chinese indicated that they were prepared to make such a concession in exchange for Indian agreement to their territorial claims in Jammu-Kashmir.

The Chinese Government concluded a Treaty of Friendship and Non-aggression with Burma after the boundary settlement, in January 1960, but, as has been seen, Burma at this time appeared to be more susceptible to pressures from China because of the weakening in India's position, which implied that India would be unlikely to extend support if Burma were threatened by Chinese Communist military action. Meanwhile the continued presence in north-eastern Burma of small groups of Chinese Nationalist forces who had crossed over from Yunnan in 1949-50 remained an issue which could excuse Chinese Communist demands for permission to send military units into Burma so as to eliminate that potential threat to China's border security. There were reports during 1961 that Burma had made some concessions on this matter to the Chinese Communist regime.

In 1954 the threat of Chinese Communist direct aggression through Indochina, in conjunction with expansion by the Communist regime in North Vietnam, was the main reason for the support given to SEATO by Thailand and the Philippines. Thailand in particular had an immediate interest in the security of Laos, Cambodia and South Vietnam. The strategic interests of the Philippines were wider, extending into the Far East on account of sensitivity to the threat which would result from Chinese Communist control of Taiwan. For Pakistan, on the other hand, membership of SEATO was to a large extent a matter of improving her position against India, especially in connection with the Kashmir dispute. This attitude persisted, but during 1960 there was a notable improvement in Pakistan's relations with India, and Pakistan proposed that the two countries should undertake joint defence measures for the security of their northern borders; this, however, was rejected by India.

The establishment of Communist power over the greater part of Laos in 1961 adversely affected Thailand's strategic position and seemed likely to further prejudice that position by contributing to subversion in Cambodia and South Vietnam. For these reasons, as has been seen, Thailand evidently felt some compulsion to move towards neutrality. At the same time, Pakistan's interest in the security of South-East Asia had evidently been reduced, and the Pakistan Government was being obliged to devote more attention to the Soviet-supported Afghan irredentist campaign directed at the Pushtu-speaking border peoples of West Pakistan.

Malaya, although she has declined membership in SEATO,

119

has shown strong interest in the security of South-East Asia against the dangers of direct Chinese Communist aggression. Malaya is associated with the Western alliance system in Asia through a defence agreement with Britain which has permitted the stationing of British Commonwealth forces within her territories. Meanwhile, through her participation with Thailand and the Philippines in the Association of South-East Asian States, Malaya is now in a position to contribute to the building up of a regional grouping which, although "non-political," may provide the economic infra-structure of an informal alliance.

In the Far East the potentially most important Asian response to the military challenge presented by China has come from Japan. Japan's rearmament, however, has been on a small scale and she has regarded her alliance with the USA as relating exclusively to her own security. Strong political opposition within Japan has been partly responsible for the slow pace of her rearmament, and sensitivity to the Sino-Soviet military threat has disposed her Governments to avoid provocation to the Communist powers.

Japan accepted a Mutual Security Treaty with the USA on a very unequal basis immediately after regaining her independence in 1951. When revised in 1960 this Treaty gave Japan some degree of equality with the USA, and in particular provided for joint consultations before any changes were to be made in the deployment or armament of US forces in Japan. The revised Treaty obligated joint counteraction in the event of an attack on the forces of either party within the territory of Japan and for this reason Japanese public opinion has been seriously disturbed at the possibility of involvement in a war against China resulting from hostilities in the Taiwan Straits.

Over recent years successive Japanese Governments have reaffirmed their desire to remain allied with the USA but they have given very little political support to overall US efforts to contain Communism in the Far East. Instead, these Governments have given indications of wishing to move towards partial neutrality: although official relations with the Chinese Communist Government have been avoided, this has been presented as compliance with US Far Eastern policies and not endorsed as a principle. Meanwhile, considerable unofficial Japanese efforts have been made to promote trade with China and extensive popular contacts with that country have been permitted. Japan's expectations of building up extensive trade with China, however, which were an important factor in modifying her co-operation for mutual security with the USA, have been dampened since 1958 by realisation of the extent to which Chinese Communist trade policy has been subordinate to political aims. Meanwhile Japan's commerce with and investments in South and South-East Asia have greatly expanded, and she may therefore develop interest in the security of those regions.

Western Responses

Western responses to the challenges presented by China have been primarily concerned with those of a military nature, but increasing attention has also been given to the problem of defeating Communist subversion in South and South-East Asia. Emphasis on meeting the danger of direct Chinese Communist aggression developed immediately after the opening of the Korean War, and was responsible for the US decision to protect the Chinese Nationalist Government on Taiwan; the Chinese Communist authorities had indicated their intention of seizing the island, and this would have weakened the US strategic position in Asia. After the armistice in Korea, Western and especially US attention shifted to the insecure situation in Indochina. There, increasing Chinese Communist military support to the struggle of the Communist-led nationalist movement against oppressive French rule seemed likely to result not only in the establishment of Communist control throughout Indochina but also in the subversion or conquest of the remainder of continental South-East Asia.

Following the 1954 Geneva agreements the USA, Britain and France sponsored the South-East Asia Collective Defence Treaty, in order to prevent further Communist expansion in the region, but France's role in this alliance became less and less significant as a result of the withdrawal of her forces from Indochina and the acquisition of genuine independence by South Vietnam, Cambodia and Laos. The USA and Britain thus became the only

Western states significantly involved in the security of the non-Communist Asian countries.

In the Far East, the USA has had an exclusive role, in virtue of her Mutual Security Agreements with Japan, South Korea and Taiwan, under which she has maintained strong military power in those countries. In South-East Asia the security role of the USA has been predominant, but a significant measure of responsibility for security in this region has been accepted by Britain through her support for SEATO and her Defence Agreement with Malaya.

The Western alliance system has been sufficiently comprehensive in the Far East, although no attempts have been made to set up a regional organisation, presumably because this would not be feasible in view of Japan's attitude. A collective security arrangement in this region might not, of course, be regarded as desirable by the USA; it would in particular reduce the USA's ability to keep limited any conflict which might develop in the Far East, and it would imply some reduction in the scope for US initiative in the region by giving the other members of such an alliance opportunities to influence its decisions.

In South-East Asia the Western alliance system is on a collective basis, instead of resulting simply from geographically related bi-lateral arrangements, but is broken by areas of neutrality and its operation is hampered by the difficulties of securing unanimity among all its members, and especially because of the lack of interest behind the French commitment. This system has no standing forces but highly mobile US striking power in the Philippines and elsewhere in the Pacific constitutes a formidable deterrent to Chinese direct aggression in South-East Asia.

The strength of the US deterrent, however, has made it inappropriate for meeting the dangers of *indirect* aggression in Asia. Precipitating a major war with China has been considered too great a price to pay for meeting such dangers, and the USA has therefore found it necessary to build up capabilities for deploying small armed units with conventional weapons in support of Asian Governments threatened by insurgent Communist action. But because the introduction of even small US forces in countries adjacent to China might provoke large-scale Chinese Communist intervention on behalf of the local Communists, the USA has felt it increasingly important to strengthen the armed forces of her Asian allies, since these have the potential to defeat attempts at indirect aggression without offering excuse for massive Chinese Communist participation. Focus on the problem of indirect aggression, however, has also resulted in clearer realisation that the effectiveness of allied Asian forces must depend on their being committed to political and economic systems which can inspire strong loyalties: such forces cannot be expected to face sacrifices in defence of corrupt and oppressive administrations. Hence greater urgency has been attached to the West's role in promoting social and political reforms while assisting economic progress in South-East Asia.

Meanwhile, in order to sustain the existing alliance system in South-East Asia, the USA has been obliged to cope with the problem of neutrality in the region. Under the Eisenhower administration, the neutral Asian countries were regarded with some disdain, especially because of the way in which some of their leaders in effect discouraged other Asian states from co-operating with the West against China, and made it easier for China to conduct her diplomacy of "peaceful co-existence."

Critics of that US attitude argued for respect of and co-operation with the governments in the neutral Asian countries, which were frequently presented as being more genuinely democratic and less corrupt than those of the West's Asian allies, as well as less vulnerable to Communist subversion. It was also argued that, because the neutral Asian governments had cordial relations with China, Western co-operation with them, together with less emphasis of military precautions against Chinese expansion, would relax tensions in Asia. Since the neutral Asian countries had links with other non-aligned states in Africa and the Middle East, moreover, it was pointed out that the West had to secure their friendship in the general interests of political strategy against the Communist bloc. After 1958, however, China's hostility towards India and her resentful criticisms of Indonesia destroyed hopes that the West might be able to promote better relations with her by working through the Asian neutrals. Moreover it was

Communist China's Foreign Policy

no longer feasible for those neutrals to recommend non-alignment to the West's Asian allies.

An indulgent attitude towards Asian neutralism has developed under the new US administration of President Kennedy. The non-alignment of those countries is now respected and their efforts to preserve it are given support. This implies abandonment of attempts to draw such countries into the Western alliance system, but it means providing them with more and more assistance to resist inducements and pressures from the Communist bloc. In this way the Asian neutrals are being encouraged to give a pro-Western orientation to their non-alignment.

A serious difficulty about the new deference towards the Asian neutrals, however, is that it encourages restlessness among the West's allies, whose governments tend to feel that they must demonstrate that their friendship cannot be taken for granted. Complaints on this basis were being made by Pakistan, Thailand and the Philippines about the economic assistance provided to the neutral Asian countries under the Eisenhower administration, and the Western commitments of increased economic aid to India in mid-1961 caused further resentment in Pakistan. For the West, a way out of the difficulty may be found in the encouragement of schemes for economic co-operation in the area, such as the Association of South-East Asian States, which has been mentioned previously. The formation of a strong community of economic interests in South and South-East Asia, cutting across existing divisions between neutral and aligned Asian countries, would improve the security of the neutrals, while focusing the attention of all members more and more on the economic grouping's own potential for economic advancement, and less and less on the need to compete individually for Western assistance.

The West has thus far given little encouragement to economic co-operation among the under-developed Asian countries although it is clear that their industrial and agricultural advancement would be accelerated by building up trade in foods, raw materials, fuels and light industrial products among themselves, and, on that basis, maximising their imports of capital goods from the advanced countries. Such economic co-operation doubtless would represent a threat to the established pattern of

124

Western exports to those countries. Domestic pressures may thus make it difficult for most Western governments to support schemes of regional co-operation in South and South-East Asia, but the West and in particular the USA cannot afford to ignore the potential for economic development and—indirectly, political stability—which would be inherent in such ventures.

Relatively large-scale Western — mostly US — aid has thus far been provided to allied and neutral Asian countries in order to promote their industrial and agricultural development on a scale which would diminish responses to the appeal of Communism. In general, however, this aid has not been extended to a degree which would bring those countries to self-sustaining growth within a reasonable period; it has simply contributed to rates of progress with uncertain promises of reaching such growth within the late 1960's. Moreover this aid has manifestly fallen short of the expectations and in many cases the absorptive capacity of those countries, and, as a result, they have had incentives to look for additional assistance from the Communist bloc.

Meanwhile, Western economic assistance to the under-developed Asian countries has not been accompanied by any substantial efforts to assist them in their trading problems: most of them are heavily dependent on fluctuating incomes from the export of fairly small ranges of primary products, and the terms of trade for those products have been declining seriously. Although these countries must depend largely on revenue from such commerce to finance their industrialisation, the West has consistently preferred to aid their economic development by loans and grants, instead of by undertaking commitments which would give those countries larger and more stable returns from their primary exports.

Pressure for social and political reform in the recipient states is now intended to be a feature of US foreign aid policy but extreme caution is evidently being shown in dealing with the established administrations, especially in neutral countries. Meanwhile, because this principle is tied to a preference for countries with high absorptive capacities, it is evidently resulting in some withdrawal from the problems of insecure countries with disorganised economies, such as Burma and Indonesia. In these two examples, the West has experienced much competition from Soviet economic assistance, which has been manifestly intended to have a strong popular impact, unrelated to needs for reform.

In so far as the new US aid policy emphasises the application of pressure for political reform, its operation may be precarious in relation to countries under strongly autocratic governments, e.g., Pakistan, Thailand, South Vietnam, and Indonesia; any attempts to encourage such administrations to share out the political power which they have concentrated so much in their own hands may provoke adverse reactions. Hence, for strategic reasons, there is likely to be continued compromise with the practical requirements of dealing with those governments as they are. Even in relations with fairly representative governments in South and South-East Asia the USA has had relatively little scope to encourage more responsible administration; there has been little opportunity for external influence to remedy the lack of real support for established social and political groups, and administrative reform has likewise been dependent mainly on internal action.

It cannot be represented, however, that the West, and in particular the USA, has altogether appropriate solutions for the political and social deficiencies of the under-developed Asian countries. Many politically conscious people in such countries are disposed to seek reform on a different basis; they have traditional moral preferences for corporate political and economic activity through consensus, with emphasis on group interests, and are consequently averse to prescriptions for democracy and progress by competitive struggles for business advantage or political power. They see a neglect of justice in Western-style "capitalism" and some doubt its ability to remedy their backwardness with the speed promised by Communism. Meanwhile, their reactions to the official aims of Western statecraft in the handling of economic assistance are adversely affected by the decadent aspects of Western civilisation, which through films and publications have a strong impact in their urban centres.

In order to overcome the vulnerabilities of the under-developed Asian countries, the West is being driven to attempt reforming action at the basic levels of civilisation and culture;

it is being obliged especially to inculcate higher standards of responsibility towards the common good. Unfortunately, however, the challenge is being presented at a time when strong disintegrating and debasing forces are at work within the West's own culture.

There are many grounds for misgivings about the ability of the West to gain respect and encourage reform in the Asian social and political systems, yet it is clear that the West will be increasingly obliged to search for ways of securing dedicated co-operation from the Asian people and that much of the success in that venture will depend on the West's own manifestations of genuine commitment to the welfare of the under-developed Asian countries. The West must not give evidence of self-seeking in the provision of its assistance to nor in its trading relations with those countries, and its mission will be compromised if the way of progress associated with its reforming action continues to lay emphasis on purely individualistic efforts towards economic development and greater democracy.

These basic problems — which still await full examination — impose certain limitations on every Western political strategy in Asia, especially in so far as they affect fundamental attitudes among the West's allies and the neutral Asian countries. This, however, does not obviate the need for adequate appraisal of the instrumental value of Western political strategies in relation to China.

Overall Western political strategy in Asia has endeavoured to counter the publicity activities undertaken by China and the Communist parties of other Asian countries, and has sought to restrict the development of China's international status. The attempts to offset Communist publicity activities in Asia have concentrated on exposing the sufferings and oppression experienced by people in the Communist countries, but, as has been seen, the West operates under certain disadvantages in competing against the nation-building appeal of Communism in Asia, especially on account of the disfavour which greets its general doctrine of progress through individualism and because the Asian peoples can find so little to admire in Western culture. The Asian countries, moreover, tend to be suspicious of Western anti-Communist propaganda simply because it is expected to be as much a reflection of selfish objectives as any other manifestation of Western foreign policies. On the other hand, the Western counter-propaganda effort has lacked vigour and initiative. In its treatment of many international issues, that effort, like much of the diplomacy of the West, has been extremely defensive. A notable example has been the failure of Western counter-propaganda to give prominence to the Communist concept of "peaceful co-existence" as a form of *struggle* in the world revolution.

The strategy of restricting the development of the Chinese Communist regime's international status has been undertaken principally by the USA, and it has been put into effect by withholding official recognition from the Chinese Communist Government and by encouraging Asian states to avoid official contact with that Government. For the USA, however, this strategy has not been a matter of simple choice. Soon after the establishment of the Chinese Communist Government, humiliating treatment of US diplomats who had remained in China and the unfavourable responses of the Chinese to a British gesture of recognition made it inadvisable for the USA to seek official relations with the Chinese Communist regime. After the outbreak of the Korean War, the US decision to protect the Chinese Nationalist Government on Taiwan was regarded by the Chinese Communists as interference in "China's" internal affairs and they affirmed that their sovereignty over that island would have to be recognised by any foreign government which wished to establish official relations with them. Since then their attitude on this question has remained unchanged and they have vehemently opposed suggestions that countries desirous of establishing diplomatic links with them might be able to do so while disputing their claim to Taiwan. It has therefore not been possible for the USA to extend recognition to the Chinese Communist regime as the effective authority on the mainland without having to face almost certain rejection of such a move — and a consequent loss of prestige in Asia.

The USA is thus virtually unable to abandon its non-recognition strategy: the real issue has become one of maintaining the strategy with the strictness that has been observed thus far or seeking to modify it by measures which, while denying potential propaganda advantages to the Chinese, would sanction unofficial contacts between the two countries, in ways which could lead to *de facto* links at the official level. The choice between these alternatives must depend on assessment of the ways in which each can help to meet the challenges from Communism in Asia.

The West must endeavour to moderate China's outlook and policies, and must eventually assist China to evolve a doctrine of nation-building based on authentic human values. This, however, is a long-term task, and it must depend largely on deep religious and cultural action outside the scope of normal diplomacy. Meanwhile, Western foreign policies must seek primarily to discourage Asian support for Communism not only by promoting economic, social and political advances in the under-developed countries, but also by resolute opposition to all forms of Communist influence and strength in Asia. Such opposition could have been possible without the non-recognition strategy if there had been no difficulties about the question of Taiwan, but the non-recognition strategy has given more effect to that opposition, and once adopted it must be continued without compromise, otherwise the resolution behind the West's attitude to Communism in Asia will appear to weaken. Strict maintenance of the non-recognition strategy is instrumental in discouraging neutral Asian compromises with Chinese and other Communist pressures, whereas relaxations of that strategy would be regarded in Asia generally as a weakening of the Western position rather than a high-principled attempt to negotiate with and exercise reforming influence on the Chinese. At the same time, relaxation of the non-recognition strategy by the USA would be regarded as evidence of the success of the Chinese Communist regime's uncompromising hostility to the West.

Some criticisms of the non-recognition strategy have stressed that it must prejudice the long-term objective of moderating China's revolutionary zeal, and that in particular it must strengthen the position of the more doctrinaire and chauvinist elements in the upper levels of the Chinese regime. It is equally arguable, however, that the position of such elements would be strengthened by any US modification of the non-recognition

129

strategy, since *prima facie* this would vindicate the doctrine of uncompromising anti-Western hostility which has reflected the strength of those elements in the Chinese system. Little is known about the existence of moderate elements in the upper levels of the Chinese Communist regime. But it seems evident that such leaders, if they form a significant group, may in some respects be in a better position as a result of continued application of the non-recognition strategy in a strict fashion, since that strategy must tend to add to the difficulties which the more doctrinaire and chauvinist Chinese leaders are presumably facing as a result of China's tensions with the Soviet Union and her increasing need to assert her interests as against the USSR.

The consequences of the US non-recognition strategy on power-struggles within the Chinese Communist regime must, of course, depend very much on the way in which that strategy is explained. It would certainly seem advantageous to present that strategy as something intended to benefit the positions of Chinese leaders with a moderate outlook and to encourage the removal of those fanatically committed to the promotion of world revolution. Explanation of the strategy as something directed against the Chinese regime simply because of its Communist nature, as has been evident in much US Far Eastern policy, undoubtedly tends to encourage anti-Communist forces in China — whose strength may be growing — but it would probably not encourage suitable responses from more moderate elements in the Chinese Communist Party. It must be repeated, of course, that there is little evidence of the existence of any moderate elements in the Chinese Communist Party and that it might be quite unreal to place hopes on encouraging them: the normal course of politics in most Communist parties has not been favourable to moderate elements; those best placed in such parties have usually been the ones with superior ability to organise, manage and intimidate their colleagues, and such individuals have usually not had moderate views.

It has been argued that less discrimination against the Chinese Communist Government would bring the USA closer to the neutral Asian states, but this view is based on a false impression of solidarity between those neutrals and the Chinese Communist regime, and on literal aceptance of their criticisms of the non-recognition strategy. Neutral Asian co-operation with China and criticisms of the non-recognition strategy have been to a considerable extent forms of conciliation intended to induce more favourable observance of "peaceful co-existence" by the Chinese. Since 1959, neutral Asian criticism of the non-recognition strategy has been reduced because of China's hostility towards India, the leading Asian neutral, and strict adherence to the non-recognition strategy must now tend to make the USA appear as a firm potential ally to neutral Asian countries which fear pressures from China. If there were any weakening in the application of that strategy such countries would see less prospect of strengthening their position by beginning co-operation with the USA. They would anticipate that the United States, for the sake of accommodation with China, might later modify its position in Asia at some cost to their own interests, even after they had partially aligned themselves with the USA; hence for the present they would be more disposed to compromise with China's demands.

Firm application of the non-recognition strategy by the United States entails dealing with the USSR as the leader of the Communist countries and in that way undoubtedly aggravates tensions in the Sino-Soviet alliance. On the one hand the USSR is probably given opportunities to neglect China's interests so as to pressure China into compliance with Soviet policy; on the other hand, China's ambitions for greater status and independence must be stimulated. It was formerly argued that by co-operating with China the West might be able to draw her away from the USSR, but this is not feasible in the present situation, because of the intensity of China's opposition to the West, and because she clearly regards such opposition as indispensable for her efforts to acquire influence in Asia.

Perseverance with the US non-recognition strategy helps to sustain the refusals of the Philippine, Malayan and Thai Governments to open diplomatic relations with the Chinese Communist regime, and, as has been seen, significant limits are thereby imposed on the opportunities for Communist expansion in those countries. Meanwhile, although the internal security aspect has little relevance to Japan's non-recognition of China, pressure against the Japanese Government to continue that strategy will probably in effect cause the Chinese to further overplay their hand by endeavouring to impose political conditions on trade between the two countries.

The absence of official contact certainly renders it difficult for the USA to negotiate with the Chinese Communist Government. The significance of this, however, can only be assessed after estimating the degree to which the Chinese are actually open to negotiation with the "imperialists." In general, the international outlook of the Chinese Communist authorities is opposed to negotiation with the West, on the grounds that any manifestation of a readiness to conclude settlements with the "imperialists" will reduce the militancy of the international Communist struggle and encourage the West to be more aggressive: uncompromising opposition must be maintained against the West in order to assure success for the global revolution. The Chinese Communist doctrine of protracted struggle, however, does sanction negotiations in order to

- disengage from conflicts or situations rendered difficult or untenable by the magnitude of actual or impending Western pressures, or
- promote divisions among the "imperialists," e.g., by favouring the USA's lesser allies, and thus inducing them to withhold support from US policies.

Meanwhile, China's national interests are clearly felt to warrant negotiations for trade or financial arrangements which will assist her economic development. China, as has been mentioned, trades with the West European countries, which for her are valuable alternative suppliers of capital goods.

Whether China is open to negotiation for purposes of disengagement, such as mentioned above, clearly depends on her prior involvement in limited wars or projects of indirect aggression, and that is something over which the West has no direct control. For the present, there can be no question of China's disengagement from external military positions, since none of her armed forces are officially located in areas outside her borders.

China would no doubt be willing to negotiate for a settlement which would mean a withdrawal of US armed forces from the Far East in exchange for pledges by her to abstain from aggression against specified countries, but assent to such an agreement would not imply any real change in her attitude towards the "imperialists," and within a short period China could be expected to resume her uncompromising opposition to the West, with allegations that the West was plotting to violate the agreement. Such opposition would be called for in order to oblige the "imperialists" to make further retreats; to assert China's ascendancy in Asia; and to discourage other Asian countries from having recourse to the West against China. It goes without saying that a US agreement to remove large forces from the Far East in exchange for non-aggression promises by the Chinese Communist Government would almost certainly be viewed by the Chinese as a spectacular confirmation of the value of unrelenting struggles against the West. Moreover, since the "imperialists" would remain "aggressive" by nature, they would plan to violate the settlement, and China would have to be prepared to use force in order to obstruct their designs. Finally—as has been illustrated by her official comments on the Korean armistice, the 1954 Geneva Agreements and on the resolution of the 1958 Middle East crisis — China would consider it essential to present any agreement for US disengagement in Asia as a retreat by the "imperialists" under pressure from the forces of international Communism, and as a gain to be extended and consolidated by further vigorous struggle against those "imperialists."

In exchange for Western disengagement from parts of South-East Asia China might also be willing to pledge non-interference in the internal affairs of South-East Asian countries which have been receiving Western protection. Such a pledge, however, would not be regarded by the Chinese as a binding renunciation of the struggle to expand Communism in Asia or of the duty of "proletarian internationalism" — the obligation to support external Communist struggles. Only in a formal sense, therefore, is China open to negotiation with the West for the conclusion of agreements that would protect South-East Asia from indirect aggression. The formal position is that the Communist powers do not engage in "indirect aggression" — they do not "export revolution" — and therefore China can without difficulty promise not to interfere in the internal affairs of the South-East Asian countries. China, however, cannot and clearly does not intend to desist from participation in the world revolution; she has long stressed that each Communist movement depends for success on the support of all other parts of the international Communist system.

China's willingness to assent to arrangements that will promote divisions between the "imperialists," together with her actual need to supplement the capital goods and manufactured products received from the Communist bloc, however, do make her open to negotiation on trade with the West European countries. In recent years her imports from those countries have greatly increased, with the result that she probably regards them as having a strong interest in persuading the USA to compromise in the face of her efforts to expand Communism in Asia. Meanwhile, China herself is apparently becoming more dependent on such trade, due to strains in her relations with the Soviet Union.

But because of the prominence which the Chinese Communist authorities have given to the Taiwan issue, and the vehemence with which they have maintained their stand on this matter, it is unlikely that they would agree to negotiate on questions of trade with the USA, in the event of the US Government taking an initiative for that purpose. If the USA modified the complete embargo which it has been maintaining on trade with China since the beginning of the Korean War, the Chinese Communist authorities would probably trade selectively with private US enterprises, along lines similar to the commerce conducted with "friendly" firms in Japan. Through such enterprises, China would then probably hope to exercise pressure for official recognition by the US Government. Meanwhile, China might, over several years, become significantly dependent on trade with the USA. The complete embargo, however, in effect supports the non-recognition strategy, and there is, therefore, a strong case for maintaining it for the sake of the immediately necessary task of encouraging resistance to Communism in Asia.

China's attitude to the question of negotiating with the "imperialists" meanwhile rules out the possibility of her agreeing to a settlement of *overall* issues with the West. Her commitment to the elimination of "imperialism" and to the establishment of world Communism is not negotiable. China must persist in her struggle against the essentially aggressive West, and in her perspective any slackening of that struggle would be to the advantage of the West and would prejudice the world revolutionary movement.

The West cannot assume that there will be any serious weakening of the ideological commitment in China's foreign policy during the immediate future, although, as has been seen, Sino-Soviet tensions increase the likelihood of important modifications in that commitment. For the present, the West must regard Chinese declarations of a readiness for overall negotiations as part of Chinese and/or Soviet strategy for the promotion of Communism, since that is the purpose assigned to such negotiations by Communist doctrine. In particular the West must note that assertions by the Communist powers of the willingness to negotiate on overall issues form part of the diplomacy of "peaceful co-existence" — which does not reflect a will for friendly relations with the West but is a form of *struggle* against the "imperialists." Through demonstrating wishes for an overall settlement with the democracies, the Communist powers intend especially to encourage more favourable neutrality among the uncommitted countries; to weaken opposition from the USA's lesser allies; and to convince all the Western nations that the Communist states have only limited external interests, with which compromise is advisable in order to avoid the risks of major conflict. Hence, while watching for evidence of real modification in her commitment to world revolution, the West must respond to any call for overall negotiations by China in ways which will contribute to the general political counter-struggle against her and against the international Communist system, and especially to defeat her search for co-operation from other Asian countries.

A call by China for overall negotiations may, of course, signify the desired change in her dedication to world Communism: that will depend on the circumstances, and the way in which it is made. Thus far such calls have been promulgated in the course of vigorous denunciations of Western "imperialism" and have in effect demanded that the West compromise with the general advance of Communism and accept "peaceful co-existence" or else face destruction. If set out in terms devoid of reference to the struggle against "imperialism," however, a Chinese offer to negotiate would be *prima facie* evidence of a genuine desire for a settlement.

Meanwhile, pending evidence of significant change in China's ideological commitment, it seems clear that the West must increase the vigour of its political counter-struggle against her. As against this it has been suggested that less Western political pressure against China would encourage favourable changes in her outlook, but, as has been seen, that — if it happened — would be a long-term affair, and it seems more likely that the actual result would be the reverse of what had been intended, since the West's moderation would be considered to vindicate the doctrine of unrelenting struggle against the "imperialists."

A more vigorous Western political counter-struggle against China can be argued for on the grounds advanced for strict application of the non-recognition strategy. Such a counter-struggle could strengthen resistance to Communism and to Chinese pressures in South and South-East Asia. Meanwhile, although it *might* provoke more intense dedication to the Communist ideology among the Chinese leaders, its successes in stiffening opposition to Communism in other parts of Asia could well produce disillusionment among those leaders. This would be all the more so if the Western counter-struggle were accompanied by notable progress towards regional co-operation for economic development in South-East Asia; if China's international position continued to be rather isolated because of her tensions with the USSR and the strains in her relations with India; and if China's economic development advanced at a slower pace because of reduced Soviet aid and further serious droughts and floods.

It has been suggested that a more vigorous political counter-struggle against China would cause the West to lose some co-operation from the neutral Asian countries. It is true that those neutrals would then see more danger of stronger Chinese displeasure if they continued their existing forms of co-operation with the West, but on account of the stiffening in Western resistance they would probably be less ready to compromise with Chinese pressures, and they would be likely to work more closely with the West if such pressures increased. Neutral Asian co-operation would certainly be attracted if China employed more inducements, but the scope for these has been seriously limited by the hard line towards India since 1958.

Prospects

Whether the challenges presented by China on her own and as a member of the international Communist system will be overcome in Asia will depend very much on the extent to which the Far Eastern and South-East Asian countries reduce their vulnerabilities by collective action and by co-operation with the West, and in particular with the USA. The required collective action must include a strengthening of the existing alliances in those areas, but it must also comprise advancement towards supranational political and economic integration in South and South-East Asia, so as to guarantee the countries of those regions more rapid economic development and greater internal security, as well as improved capabilities for meeting direct aggression.

In the immediate future Chinese Communist military superiority over the other Asian countries will undoubtedly increase. Neither Japan nor India are likely to build up their armed forces to a degree which would give them adequate protection against a Chinese Communist attack or which would enable them to accept security commitments elsewhere in Asia. Meanwhile, India is unlikely to develop interest in the security of South-East Asia, but Japan, because of the expansion of her trade and investments in that region, may well become interested in its security, especially if she joins or becomes associated with some future South-East Asian economic community. At the same time, the trend of increasing economic co-operation between Japan and India is likely to continue and this may lead to mutual support in international affairs, especially as against China. If Soviet and Chinese strategy towards Japan places more emphasis on building up large-scale trade with that country stronger trends towards neutrality in Japan's foreign policy could develop. This, however, would be a long-term affair and the record suggests that both

Communist powers would defeat their aim through over-hasty attempts to exert leverage for political concessions from Japan before the prospects for large-scale commerce would appear secure enough to the country's ruling conservative circles.

Pending substantial changes in her foreign policy, which are likely only in the long term — unless her relations with the USSR deteriorate further — China will undoubtedly continue to encourage armed revolutionary struggles by the Communist parties in South and South-East Asia. This will probably accord with Soviet wishes in the cases of Malaya and the Philippines, but possibly not in Thailand and probably not in India, Indonesia or Ceylon. Meanwhile, if China encourages and assists intensified military action by the Burmese Communist Party this will presumably be done cautiously and with as much secrecy as possible, and it may well be opposed by the USSR, because of the likely effect on India. The Soviet Union's apparent opposition to the use of violence by the Communist movements in India and Indonesia will probably continue as long as those two countries receive Soviet economic aid and adhere to neutrality, unless marked discrimination is shown against their local Communist parties, or unless the stability of their governments is seriously weakened. In the immediate future the USSR probably expects less goodwill from India's neutrality, because of the heavy increases in Western economic assistance to India and China's continued hostility to the Nehru Government, but unless India switches to alignment with the West, Soviet strategy towards her will probably continue to emphasise co-operation with the ruling Congress Party.

In the immediate future, the neutral Asian countries are not likely to make significant progress towards mutual support against the dangers presented by China. In the longer term they may be drawn into a regional economic organisation, such as the Association of South-East Asian States, and thereby become committed to an incipient alliance, but their entry into such a body will probably depend on its prior manifestation of attractive prospects for commerce and industrial development.

Of the West's Asian allies, Thailand may well adopt a partly neutral foreign policy in the hope of securing reductions in Communist pressures from Laos, but she will undoubtedly continue her membership of SEATO and endeavour to gain more extensive military and economic assistance from the USA. Pakistan's interests in the security of South-East Asia will probably be further reduced, because of preoccupation with the irredentist threat from Afghanistan and resentment at the increased favour to India in US foreign policy.

Greater responsibility for the security of South-East Asia from direct and indirect aggression will have to be accepted by the USA, since Britain's economic and strategic interests in this region will undoubtedly decline with her participation in the European Economic Community. In the long term, moreover, Britain's membership of that Community will presumably restrict her individual freedom of action in relation to security commitments in South-East Asia. Nevertheless, in the immediate future, Britain, in virtue of her powerful international position, will still be able to exercise much influence on US policies in Asia.

Meanwhile, in the short term, the USA will find it difficult to strengthen the Western alliance system in South-East Asia. France's participation in SEATO will presumably continue to be a nominal affair; vigorous economic and military assistance will have to be given to Thailand and Pakistan if their solidarity with the alliance is to be improved; and special efforts will be needed to promote effective security along Thailand's eastern borders. It is unlikely that the area of Communist control in Laos will be reduced, or that there will be any improvement in Cambodia's internal security. With increased US military assistance, however, the struggle to eliminate Viet Minh terrorists in South Vietnam will probably become more effective.

The new US diplomacy of goodwill towards the Asian neutrals will probably achieve successes, especially in the form of graduated co-operation on international issues from India. The goodwill produced by this diplomacy may prepare the way for efforts to encourage broad economic co-operation among those neutrals and with the West's Asian allies.

In the immediate future, Western and in particular US economic assistance to the South and South-East Asian countries will no doubt increase gradually, but the West is unlikely to give them much assistance in their trading problems. Those countries will thus continue to be open to Soviet and other Communist trade diplomacy and will be further attracted towards accepting economic assistance from the Communist bloc. The potential of the Association of South-East Asian States for economic development and integration will undoubtedly be realised rather slowly and this is likely to be true of any other regional organisation of this nature. Yet if ways can be found to stimulate economic advances within such a body the utility of Western economic assistance to its member countries will be raised and their interest in developmental aid from the Soviet bloc will be reduced.

In the long run the Western powers and in particular the USA may commit themselves in their foreign aid programmes to the projection of a doctrine of advancement through the building up of mixed economies, with emphasis on the promotion of social justice in the under-developed Asian countries. But for the present this is unlikely; for domestic reasons, the USA especially may find it difficult to advocate strong public sector development in the backward Asian economies. Yet increasing awareness of the urgency of more rapid economic progress in those countries may in practice result in greater emphasis by Western aid policy on accelerated development of fuel, power, transport and other infrastructure industries as public enterprises, more or less on the Indian pattern.

The West cannot anticipate any slackening of China's protracted struggle for the expansion of Communism, but must be prepared to meet sharper opposition from her, since the ideological commitment in her foreign policy is likely to become more chauvinist. Yet while the need for political and military resistance to China and to Asian Communism generally may well increase, the West will also be obliged to accept more fully the challenge to competition in nation-building which China projects in Asia. Through giving reparation for all that the under-developed Asian countries endured under Western colonial rule, and through building up a profound solidarity with those countries, assistance in that nation-building has the promise of being the more noble, the more decisive and the more enduring part of the West's response to China's foreign policy. In the long term, the West's contribution to nation-building in South and South-East Asia may also inspire the Chinese leaders to seek in a more human political philosophy the ideals of justice and fraternity which have been invoked so powerfully and yet distorted so tragically by Communism. And, while obliging the Western nations to strive for this purpose, history may later make it possible for them to make amends for those humiliations of the 19th century which have represented such a plausible case for China's contemporary hostility to "imperialism."

Selected Bibliography

ABBAS, S. A. *Capital Requirements for the Development of South and South-East Asia.* New York: Gregory Lounz, 1955.

ADLER, SOLOMON. *The Chinese Economy.* New York: Modern Review Press, 1957.

AGARAWALA, A. N., and SINGH, S. P. (eds.). *The Economics of Underdevelopment.* London and New York: Oxford University Press, 1958.

ALLEN, ROBERT LORING. *Soviet Economic Warfare.* Washington, D.C.: Public Affairs Press, 1960.

ALMOND, GABRIEL A., and COLEMAN, JAMES S. *The Politics of the Developing Areas.* Princeton, N.J.: Princeton University Press, 1960.

BARNETT, A. DOAK. *Communist China and Asia.* New York: Harper & Brothers, 1960.

BOORMAN, HOWARD L., and others. *Moscow-Peking Axis: Strengths and Strains.* New York: Harper & Brothers, 1957.

BRIMMELL, J. H. *Communism in South East Asia: A Political Analysis.* London and New York: Oxford University Press, 1959.

BRZEZINSKI, ZBIGNIEW K. *The Soviet Bloc.* New York: Frederick A. Praeger, 1961.

BUTWELL, RICHARD. *Southeast Asia Today—And Tomorrow.* New York: Frederick A. Praeger, 1961.

CHANDRA-SEKHAR, SRIPATI. *Red China: An Asian View.* New York: Frederick A. Praeger, 1961.

EMERSON, RUPERT. *Representative Government in Southeast Asia.* Cambridge, Mass.: Harvard University Press, 1955.

FIFIELD, RUSSELL H. *The Diplomacy of Southeast Asia: 1945–1958.* New York: Harper & Brothers, 1958.

FITZGERALD, C. P. *Revolution in China.* London: The Cresset Press, 1952.

HARRISON, SELIG S. (ed.). *India and the United States.* New York: The Macmillan Company, 1961.

HU, CHANG-TU, and others. *China: Its People, Its Society, Its Culture.* Human Relations Area Files. New York: Taplinger Publishing Co., 1959.

HUDSON, G. F., LOWENTHAL, RICHARD and MACFARQUHAR, RODERICK. *The Sino-Soviet Dispute.* New York: Frederick A. Praeger, 1961.

Selected Bibliography

HUGHES, T. J., and LUARD, D. E. T. *The Economic Development of Communist China, 1949–1958*. London and New York: Oxford University Press, 1959.

JORDAN, AMOS A., JR. *Foreign Aid and the Defense of Southeast Asia*. New York: Frederick A. Praeger, 1962.

KAHIN, GEORGE MCTURNAN (ed.). *Major Governments of Asia*. Ithaca, N.Y.: Cornell University Press, 1958.

KENNEDY, MALCOLM D. *A History of Communism in East Asia*. New York: Frederick A. Praeger, 1957.

KIRBY, E. S. "Foreign Policy of Communist China," *International Journal*, XV, No. 1.

LABIN, SUZANNE. *The Anthill: The Human Condition in Communist China*. New York: Frederick A. Praeger, 1960.

LENG, SHAO-CHUAN. *Japan and Communist China*. New York: Institute of Pacific Relations, 1958.

———, and PALMER, NORMAN D. *Sun Yat-sen and Communism*. New York: Frederick A. Praeger, 1960.

LEVENSON, JOSEPH R. *Confucian China and Its Modern Fate: The Problem of Intellectual Continuity*. Berkeley, Calif.: University of California Press, 1958.

LINDSAY, MICHAEL. *China and the Cold War*. Melbourne: Melbourne University Press, 1955.

LINEBARGER, PAUL M. A., DJANG, CHU, and BURKS, ARDATH W. *Far Eastern Governments and Politics: China and Japan* (2d ed.). Princeton, N.J.: D. Van Nostrand Company, 1956.

LONDON, KURT L. *Unity and Contradiction: Major Aspects of Sino-Soviet Relations*. New York: Frederick A. Praeger, 1962.

MACFARQUHAR, RODERICK. *The Hundred Flowers Campaign and the Chinese Intellectuals*. New York: Frederick A. Praeger, 1960.

MICHAEL, FRANZ H., and TAYLOR, GEORGE E. *The Far East in the Modern World*. New York: Henry Holt & Co., 1956.

NORTH, ROBERT C. *Moscow and the Chinese Communists*. Berkeley, Calif.: University of California Press, 1953.

ROSTOW, W. W. *Prospects for Communist China*. New York: John Wiley & Sons, 1954.

SHABAD, THEODORE. *China's Changing Map: A Political and Economic Geography of the Chinese People's Republic*. New York: Frederick A. Praeger, 1956.

STEINER, H. ARTHUR. *The International Position of Communist China*. New York: Institute of Pacific Relations, 1958.

Selected Bibliography

TANG, PETER S. H. *Communist China Today*. New York: Frederick A. Praeger, 1957.

THORNTON, T. P. "Peking, Moscow and the Underdeveloped Areas," *World Politics*, XIII, No. 3.

THAYER, PHILIP W. (ed.). *Nationalism and Progress in Free Asia*. Baltimore, Md.: The Johns Hopkins Press, 1956.

TINKER, HUGH. *The Union of Burma*. London and New York: Oxford University Press, 1959.

TRAGER, FRANK N. (ed.). *Marxism in Southeast Asia: A Study of Four Countries*. Stanford, Calif.: Stanford University Press, 1959.

VANDENBOSCH, AMRY, and BUTWELL, R. A. *Southeast Asia Among the World Powers*. Lexington, Ky.: University of Kentucky Press, 1958.

VINACKE, HAROLD M. *Far Eastern Politics in the Postwar Period*. New York: Appleton-Century-Crofts, 1956.

WALKER, RICHARD L. *The Continuing Struggle*. New York: The Bookmailer, 1958.

WEI, HENRY. *China and Soviet Russia*. Princeton, N.J.: D. Van Nostrand Company, 1956.

WOLF, C., JR. *Foreign Aid: Theory and Practice in Southern Asia*. Princeton, N.J.: Princeton University Press, 1960.

Index

145

Index

146

Index